# Understanding the Synod on Synodality, 2023 Session

# Understanding the Synod on Synodality, 2023 Session

A Community of Mutual Empowerment

JAMES CHUKWUMA OKOYE

*Foreword by Fortunatus Nwachukwu*

WIPF & STOCK · Eugene, Oregon

UNDERSTANDING THE SYNOD ON SYNODALITY, 2023 SESSION
A Community of Mutual Empowerment

Copyright © 2024 James Chukwuma Okoye. All rights reserved. Except for brief quotations in critical publications or reviews, no part of this book may be reproduced in any manner without prior written permission from the publisher. Write: Permissions, Wipf and Stock Publishers, 199 W. 8th Ave., Suite 3, Eugene, OR 97401.

Wipf & Stock
An Imprint of Wipf and Stock Publishers
199 W. 8th Ave., Suite 3
Eugene, OR 97401

www.wipfandstock.com

PAPERBACK ISBN: 979-8-3852-2436-4
HARDCOVER ISBN: 979-8-3852-2437-1
EBOOK ISBN: 979-8-3852-2438-8

09/19/24

*Imprimi potest*
Very Rev. Fr. Chris Christy, C.S.Sp.
Provincial, Spiritan Province, USA

Images and photos of the synod by permission of the Secretariat of the Synod of Bishops

Unless otherwise indicated, the Holy Scripture is cited according the text of the *New American Bible, Revised Edition*, 2011.

*Dedicated to Pope Francis, Man of the Spirit, Apostle of Divine Mercy*

# Contents

| | | |
|---|---|---|
| | *List of Images* | ix |
| | *Foreword by Fortunatus Nwachukwu* | xi |
| | *Preface* | xv |
| | *Abbreviations* | xvii |
| | *Letter from Cardinal Mario Grech* | xix |
| 1 | Paradigms of Synodality | 1 |
| 2 | Theological Footprints toward the Synod on Synodality | 7 |
| 3 | Canonical Footprints toward the Synod on Synodality | 20 |
| 4 | The Documents of the 2023 Synod | 36 |
| 5 | The Documents: *Instrumentum laboris* | 49 |
| 6 | Discordant Voices on the Synod on Synodality | 69 |
| 7 | Participation in the Synod 2023 Session | 75 |
| 8 | The *Dubia* Cardinals and the Pope's Response | 78 |
| 9 | The Opening Retreat | 81 |
| 10 | The Synod Assembly | 85 |
| 11 | Synod Letter to the People of God and Context of the *Synthesis Report* | 102 |
| 12 | The *Synthesis Report* with Commentary | 108 |
| 13 | Toward the October 2024 Assembly | 128 |
| 14 | Evaluations of the 2023 Synod Experience | 131 |
| 15 | Conclusion | 135 |
| | *Bibliography* | 141 |
| | *Index* | 149 |

# List of Images

Image 1. Delegates at synod round tables   3
Image 2. Undersecretaries of the Synod Secretariat: Bp. Luis Marín de San Martín, OSA and Sr. Nathalie Becquart   28
Image 3. Conversation in the Spirit (diagram)   53
Image 4. Fr. Timothy Radcliffe, OP, preacher of the synod retreat   83
Image 5. Pope Francis at his synod round table   86
Image 6. Cardinal Jean-Claude Hollerich, SJ, Relator of the Synod   89
Image 7. Cardinal Mario Grech, OSA, General Secretary of the Synod of Bishops   101

# Foreword

LIFE IS A JOURNEY. For us Christians, it is a journey back to God. God is forever calling us to leave the death-dealing world in which we may feel comfortable and to set forth on a path that will take us back to him. This is why the metaphor of journey lies at the heart of the Sacred Scriptures and serves as an overarching framework in them. The Bible is filled with many journey stories which testify to this reality—the journey of Abraham, the Exodus, the return from exile in Babylon, the journey of Joseph and Mary to Bethlehem, their flight into Egypt, the journey of Jesus from Galilee to Jerusalem, the Emmaus story, the ceaseless travels of Saint Paul from one place to another, and so on. The list could go on almost indefinitely. The journey could sometimes be uncomfortable, even painful, but it is the only way into the fullness of life in God, who loved us into life and who is the author and determiner of destinies on earth.

If the Christian life is a journey back to God, it means that the Church—the community of the entire People of God—is also on a journey. As Pope Francis said in his address on the fiftieth anniversary of the Synod of Bishops on October 17, 2015, the Church is "nothing other than the 'journeying together' of God's flock along the paths of history towards the encounter with Christ the Lord."[1] The term *synod* is used to refer to this "journeying together" of all the People of God, from the bishop to the last of the faithful. Therefore, the Church is intrinsically synodal and synodality is a constitutive element of the Church. To be synodal means to be together on the way. It entails a communal sharing of space and life, walking and running together, in shared respect for the differing paces and energies, as in the Easter morning race of Peter and the beloved disciple of Jesus (John 20:1–10). It also entails listening to one another; a mutual listening

---

1. Francis, "Address at the Ceremony."

in which everyone—the faithful people of God, the bishops (the bishop of Rome included)—has something to learn.

From April 10 to May 8, 1994, the First Special Assembly for Africa of the Synod of Bishops, also colloquially called the First African Synod, was held in Rome. The topic was "The Church in Africa and Her Evangelizing Mission Towards the Year 2000: 'You shall be my witnesses (Acts 1:8).'" The synodal gathering was preceded by a long period of preparation, guided by a preliminary document or *Lineamenta*. Professor James Chukwuma Okoye, CSSp, was a major contributor to the work that produced that document, and he followed the preparatory process until its consummation at the special assembly. That experience certainly shaped and enriched his knowledge of the synod and synodal processes.

This volume, *Understanding the Synod on Synodality, 2023 Session: A Community of Mutual Empowerment*, has therefore been written by someone who has a clear knowledge of his subject and is passionate about it. The book offers an insightful reflection on synod and synodality, presented with the depth and thoroughness of a seasoned scholar. The contents of the book testify to a great work accomplished. They are remarkably exhaustive and weave together an enormous amount of information drawn from official magisterial documents of the Church, including writings and preachings of the popes, documents of the Roman Curia, canonical and historical texts, as well as contributions of individual authors related to the theme of synod and synodality. Professor Okoye presents and analyzes these materials both singularly and in relationship with the synodal initiative launched by Pope Francis. All this makes of this book an attractive treasure of historical, ecclesial, canonical, and magisterial teachings, expounded and presented with exceptional biblical skills.

Anyone desirous of understanding the meaning and intricacies of synod and synodality will find this book very helpful. Beyond the amazing quantity of information contained in the book, its elaborate bibliography and footnotes also offer the reader access to texts that are either little known or have been relegated to oblivion. The book surely provides a standpoint for further reflections. It is a promise that more will surely be written, spoken, and achieved. It is both a testimony to the past and a pledge to a mission to be completed.

A special touch has been brought to this book by the academic background of the author, a biblical scholar and professor emeritus of Old Testament studies. Professor Okoye is certainly one of the best African biblical scholars with a profound and outstanding knowledge of Hebrew and the other Semitic languages. Many ecclesiastical institutions have benefited from his gifts, and he has been a distinguished academic and personality among biblical scholars, who see him chiefly as one who has the capacity to grapple with biblical sources and interpret them in an enriching way to the contemporary reader. Professor Okoye's talents lie not only in his vast knowledge, but also in his capacity to share it in simple, accessible language, and this is at the heart of why many consider him a born teacher. In this book he brings his natural talents and acquired skills to service in meticulously gleaning from diverse sources an amazing quantity of information, which he synthesizes and presents to the author's relish.

For Professor Okoye's devotees and for the casual reader too, this volume will serve as a timely reminder not only of his abilities, but also of the things he holds dear, to which he has dedicated his life and for which he has been prepared to sacrifice and fight. We thank him and pray that his words, both written and spoken, may continue to be for us a rich treasure of teaching and witness for many years to come.

FORTUNATUS NWACHUKWU
Secretary
Dicastery for Evangelization
Section for First Evangelization
and New Local Churches

# Preface

I WORKED IN THE Synod of Bishops for the first Synod of Bishops for Africa. So I knew all about the synod. The term *synodality*, however, was a challenge at first; it was not in common parlance until, in the wake of Pope Francis and his desire for a synodal church, the International Theological Commission published a study of it in March 2018. Synodality was an ancient practice that lapsed somewhat in the Latin Church, though preserved in some form in the Eastern Orthodox Church.

Pope Francis was ordained a Jesuit priest on December 13, 1969, that is, after Vatican II (1962–65). Two experiences seem to drive his quest for a synodal church. The first is the 1985 Extraordinary Synod's synthesis of the themes of Vatican II in the concept of *communio*. This caught the imagination of the church, and *communio* ecclesiology proliferated. The second and more personal, his participation in the assemblies of CELAM (Latin American Episcopal Council), which since the Second Episcopal Conference of Latin America (Medellin, 1968) practiced synodality without naming it as such. Pope Francis was especially marked by the Assembly of Aparecida (May 2007), the text of which he was the principal redactor. His very first encyclical, *Evangelii gaudium, The Joy of the Gospel* (November 24, 2013), resonates with Aparecida themes and already contained the seeds of what would germinate as the synod on synodality. The occasion of the fiftieth anniversary of the Synod of Bishops (October 17, 2015) gave him the opportunity to tease out some of the themes of synodality. And he wasted no time translating some synodal ideals into law—the reform of the Roman Curia with his Apostolic Constitution *Praedicate evangelium, On the Roman Curia and Its Service to the Church and to the World* (March 19, 2022) was a significant step in this direction.

## PREFACE

This book follows, stage by stage, the footprints of the church as *communio*, showing this blossoming into synodality and the synodal church.[2] I discuss the theological footprints, beginning with Vatican II, then the canonical. I briefly review the documents for the October 2023 synod before outlining the actual process of the assembly itself. The *Synthesis Report*, though not the final document of the synod on synodality, receives close attention as enshrining the fruits of the process so far. As I researched this book, it became clear that the synod on synodality advances the reception and necessary updating of Vatican II, especially in the pastoral and process fields.

I accessed whatever was openly available at synod.va, the website of the Secretariat of the Synod of Bishops. The response (below) to my letter to the Cardinal Secretary of the Synod of Bishops makes clear why some materials are for the meantime on embargo.

---

2. The second phrase in the title of this book, "A Community of Mutual Empowerment," is taken from the fifth session of the retreat by Fr. Radcliffe (see chapter 9, below).

# Abbreviations

| | |
|---|---|
| *AL* | Post-Synodal Apostolic Exhortation, *Amoris laetitia, On Love in the Family*, March 19, 2016 |
| CCEO | Code of Canon Law for Eastern Catholic Churches |
| CDF | Congregation for Doctrine of the Faith |
| CELAM | Latin American Episcopal Council (*Consejo Episcopal Latinoamericano y Caribeño*) |
| CIC | Code of Canon Law |
| *CL* | John Paul II, Post-Synodal Apostolic Exhortation, *Christifideles laici*, September 30, 1988 |
| *DCS* | *Working Document for the Continental Stage* |
| DDF | Dicastery for the Doctrine of the Faith |
| *EC* | Pope Francis, Apostolic Constitution *Episcopalis communio, On the Synod of Bishops*, September 15, 2018 |
| *EG* | Pope Francis, Encyclical, *Evangelii gaudium, The Joy of the Gospel*, 2013 |
| *EN* | Paul VI, Apostolic Exhortation, *Evangelii nuntiandi*, December 8, 1975 |
| Ep. Conf. | Episcopal Conference |
| *IL* | *Instrumentum laboris*, October 2023 Synod |
| ITC | International Theological Commission |
| *PD* | *Preparatory Document for the 16th General Assembly of the Synod of Bishops: For a Synodal Church: Communion, Participation, and Mission*, September 7, 2021 |

## ABBREVIATIONS

| | |
|---|---|
| PE | Pope Francis, Apostolic Constitution, *Praedicate evangelium, On the Roman Curia and Its Service to the Church and to the World*, March 19, 2022 |
| SECAM | Symposium of the Episcopal Conferences of Africa and Madagascar |
| SR | *Synthesis Report, A Synodal Church in Mission*, October 28, 2023 |
| TDNT | *Theological Dictionary of the New Testament* |
| Handbook | *Vademecum for the Synod on Synodality: Official Handbook for Listening and Discernment in Local Churches* |

## DOCUMENTS OF THE VATICAN II

| | |
|---|---|
| AA | *Apostolicam Actuositatem*, Decree on the Apostolate of the Laity |
| AG | *Ad gentes*, Decree on the Missionary Activity of the Church |
| CD | *Christus Dominus*, Decree on the Bishops' Pastoral Office in the Church |
| DV | *Dei verbum*, Dogmatic Constitution on Divine Revelation |
| GS | *Gaudium et spes*, Dogmatic Constitution on the Church in the Modern World |
| LG | *Lumen gentium*, Dogmatic Constitution on the Church |
| UR | *Unitatis redintegratio*, Decree on Ecumenism |

SECRETARIA GENERALIS
SYNOD!

Vatican, 18 March 2024
Prot. N. 240061

Dear Fr. Okoye,

Thank you for your letter of 15 January in which you describe your book project for the Synod on Synodality. The outline you attached is indeed impressive. You have also asked for access to documentation that is contained in our archives: for example, the summaries of the daily work of the *circuli minores*, the general addresses *in aula*, and the draft from which the *Synthesis report* emerged. I regret to inform you that for the moment the acts of the synodal assembly are confidential.

Thank you for the generosity with which you are documenting the journey on which Pope Francis is leading the entire Church. Your book will be an invaluable resource. Thank you also for your kind understanding of my concern for the integrity of this process through its completion.

As we walk this Lenten journey of conversion, I avail myself of this opportunity to ask for your prayers and assure you of mine.

Mario Card. GRECH
*General Secretary*


To the Rev. Father James Chukwuma Okoye,
CSSp Director, Center for Spiritan Studies
Duquesne University
600 Forbes Avenue, Trinity Hall Pittsburgh, PA 15282 U.S.A.

Via della Conciliazione, 34-00120 Citta del Vaticano
Tel.: (+39) 06 698.84324/84821—Fax: (+39) 06 698.83392
E-mail: synodus @synod.va Internet: https://www.synod.va

# 1

# Paradigms of Synodality

## SYNOD

THE WORD SYNOD DERIVES from two Greek words, *sun* ("with, together") and *hodos* ("way, journey"). It signifies the assembling and journeying together of the local churches. The early church met in synods, a practice preserved in the Eastern Orthodox Churches. Until Vatican II and even in the Vatican II documents themselves, *synodus* (synod) and *concilium* (council) were used interchangeably. When Vatican II reached consensus on collegiality, the College of Bishops with and under the Head of the College, Pope Paul VI, with his motu proprio *Apostolica sollicitudo, Establishing the Synod of Bishops for the Universal Church*, September 15, 1965, reestablished the synod of bishops in the Catholic Church as a "special permanent council of bishops" (preamble). This provision was then inserted into the final draft of *Christus Dominus* (henceforth *CD*), no. 5, October 28, 1965. Henceforth, synod became distinct from council.

The Synod of Bishops is codified in canons 342–348 (1983 Code) and the Code of Canons of the Eastern Churches (1990), canon 46. The pope convokes the synod and sets the agenda. The attending bishops represent and act in the name of the entire Catholic episcopate. The synod is consultative, but may enjoy deliberative power, should the Roman pontiff grant this (1983 Code, canon 337.2). It meets in Ordinary, Extraordinary, and

Special Assemblies.[1] The norms of the Synod of Bishops have seen constant updating,[2] the most recent being Pope Francis' Apostolic Constitution *Episcopalis communio, On the Synod of Bishops* (September 15, 2018).

The Synod of Bishops is "in some manner the image" of an ecumenical council and reflects its "spirit and method."[3] It has proven to be a privileged instrument for the implementation of Vatican II. In 1983, Pope John Paul II could say, "The synodal key for the reading of the council's text became, so to say, a place for the interpretation, application, and further development of Vatican II."[4]

## SYNODALITY

Pope Francis declared synodality a "constitutive element of the Church."[5] On October 9–10, 2021, he convoked the synod on synodality to meet in October 2023 as the 16th Ordinary General Assembly of the Synod of Bishops. The topic of synodality had come second, after priests, in the pope's survey of the bishops of the world for their preferences.[6] The process would go through three stages. The local/national stage (dioceses and bishops' conferences) opened on October 17 guided by two documents, *Preparatory Document for the 16th General Assembly of the Synod of Bishops: For a Synodal Church: Communion, Participation, and Mission* (September 7, 2021; henceforth *PD*), and *Vademecum for the Synod on Synodality: Official Handbook for Listening and Discernment in Local Churches* (henceforth *Handbook*). The Continental Stage had as guide the *Working Document for the Continental Stage* (henceforth *DCS*): "Enlarge the space of your tent, spread out your tent cloths unsparingly, lengthen your ropes and make firm your pegs" (Isa 54:2). A novelty was the Digital Synod, an online initiative

---

1. The Ordinary General Assembly meets for matters concerning the good of the universal Church; an Extraordinary General Assembly meets for matters of urgent consideration. A Special Assembly may meet for matters which mostly concern one or more specific geographical regions. The Roman pontiff may convene other synodal assemblies with other modalities established by him. See Synod of Bishops, "Profile."

2. See various editions of Paul VI, *Ordo Synodi Episcoporum*, 1966, 1969, 1971; and John Paul II, *Ordo Synodi Episcoporum*, 2006; most recently Francis, *Episcopalis communio*.

3. Francis, *Episcopalis communio*, no. 8.

4. John Paul II, "Theological Basis," no. 1.

5. Francis, "Address at the Ceremony"; see also *Episcopalis communio*, no. 6.

6. Francis, "Opening of the Works."

especially for the age group eighteen to forty.⁷ The *Synthesis Report* gathers the results of the October 4–29, 2023 session.

In his Angelus Address of October 16, 2022, Pope Francis split the Universal Stage into two sessions meeting in Rome—October 2023 and October 2024.

Unlike prior synods, the synod on synodality is not focused on specific topics,⁸ rather on the journeying together (*sun*, "with, together"; *hodos*, "way, journey") of the People of God as "a hierarchically structured community"⁹ that mutually shares the charisms of the Spirit. As Cardinal Hollerich would reiterate at the end of the 2023 session, the Synod "is about synodality . . . even if people have not believed us."¹⁰

**Delegates at synod round tables.**

Synodality translates the trinitarian dynamism with which God comes to meet humanity into spiritual attitudes and ecclesial processes.¹¹

---

7. For detail, see the testimony of Sister Xiskya Paguaga, RP and Mr. José Manuel Gonzalez at the Sixth General Congregation below.

8. The world press speculated particularly about women's ordination and acceptance of same-sex unions.

9. ITC, *Synodality in the Life and Mission*, no. 69.

10. Brockhaus, "Cardinal Hollerich," §8.

11. Synod of Bishops, *Synthesis Report*, ch. 1, a.

The protagonist of the synod is the Holy Spirit.[12] Synodality is ordered to mission; the church's synodal journey is oriented toward the Kingdom.[13]

Only two questions were on the table for this synod: "How does this 'journeying together' take place today on different levels (from the local level to the universal one), allowing the church to proclaim the Gospel? What steps is the Spirit inviting us to take in order to grow as a synodal church?"[14]

It is frankly admitted that "synodality is a term unfamiliar to many members of the People of God, causing people confusion and concern. Among the fears expressed is that the teaching of the church will be changed."[15] Synodality defines itself as:

> Christians walking in communion with Christ toward the Kingdom along with the whole of humanity. Its orientation is towards mission, and its practice involves gathering in assembly at each level of ecclesial life. It involves reciprocal listening, dialogue, community discernment, and creation of consensus as an expression that renders Christ present in the Holy Spirit, each taking decisions in accordance with their responsibilities.[16]

The International Theological Commission (henceforth ITC) adds that "synodality denotes those structures and ecclesial processes in which the synodal nature of the church is expressed at an institutional level, but analogously on various levels."[17]

## PARADIGMS OF SYNODALITY AND LESSONS FROM THE "PROTO-SYNOD"

Paradigms of the church living and acting synodally occur in the Acts of the Apostles. In the Upper Room before Pentecost, there were together Peter and the apostles, but also some women and Mary the mother of Jesus and his brothers, all devoting themselves with one accord, with one mind, purpose, or impulse to prayer (Acts 1:13–14). Upon Peter's suggestion, this

---

12. Francis, "Moment of Reflection."
13. Synod of Bishops, *Synthesis Report*, ch. 1, e and b.
14. *PD*, no. 2, and often in the synod documents.
15. Synod of Bishops, *Synthesis Report*, ch. 1, i.
16. Synod of Bishops, *Synthesis Report*, ch. 1, h.
17. ITC, *Synodality in the Life*, 70b.

group proposed two persons to replace Judas. They cast lots for them and the lot fell upon Matthias, and he was counted with the eleven apostles (Acts 1:26).

On the day of Pentecost, "they were all filled with the Holy Spirit and began to speak in different tongues as the Spirit enabled them to proclaim" (Acts 2:4).[18] After three thousand persons accepted Peter's message and were baptized, "they devoted themselves to the teaching of the apostles and to the communal life, to the breaking of the bread and to the prayers" (Acts 2:42).

Even in the life of Jesus, Luke reports a double sending out of his disciples. In Luke 9:1–6, he sent out the Twelve. In Luke 10:1–12, he "appointed seventy-two others whom he sent ahead of him in pairs to every town and place he intended to visit." Their empowering and message is similar. He sent the Twelve "to proclaim the kingdom of God and to heal [the sick]" (Luke 9:2). The seventy-two he sent to "cure the sick in it and say to them, 'The kingdom of God is at hand for you'" (Luke 10:9). The Twelve "went from village to village proclaiming the good news and curing diseases everywhere" (Luke 9:6). The seventy-two, upon return, reported, "Lord, even the demons are subject to us because of your name." To which he replied, "Behold I have given you power [*tén exousian*] to tread upon serpents and scorpions and upon the full force of the enemy" (Luke 10:17–19). The interplay of the Twelve and the other seventy-two illustrates co-responsibility in mission.

In Acts 10, the church had "the experience of the Spirit in which Peter and the early community recognize the risk of placing unjustified limits on faith sharing" (*PD*, 17b). Those who accompanied Peter to the home of Cornelius "were astounded that the gift of the Holy Spirit should have been poured out on the Gentiles also" (Acts 10:46). In Jerusalem, the circumcised believers took Peter to task, but he was able to show that he was following the lead of the Holy Spirit.[19]

The Council of Jerusalem (Acts 15) is the original model, the "protosynod." It illustrates the interconnectedness of *synodos* and *methodos* (path to reach the desired goal).[20] When Paul and Barnabas disagreed with the Judaizers about the necessity of circumcision for salvation, the Church of

---

18. Unless otherwise indicated, Scripture citations follow the *New American Bible Revised Edition* (NABRE).

19. "If then God gave them the same gift he gave to us when we came to believe in the Lord Jesus Christ, who was I to be able to hinder God?" (Acts 11:17).

20. See Schönborn, "Lessons from the Council of Jerusalem." Much in this section is indebted to him.

Antioch sent them and some of the others to the apostles and presbyters in Jerusalem. The leader of the Jerusalem Church was James, not one of the Twelve.[21] "The conflict was *expressed*. It was openly *named* and openly *dealt with* . . . . They *told stories!* They did not give some kind of theological treatise. They did not theorize abstractly about the salvation of the gentiles, but rather *described* what they had 'seen and heard.'"[22] Peter spoke about his experience with Cornelius. "The whole assembly fell silent, and they *listened* while Paul and Barnabas described the signs and wonders God had worked among the Gentiles through them" (Acts 15:13; italics mine). James summarized the discernment and suggested that gentiles not be forced to circumcise, but to observe certain precepts of the Torah in order to facilitate communion with Jewish Christians.[23] "Scripture and experience coincide. In listening to both the writings and the experience, the assembly recognizes the way and the will of God."[24] They, the apostles, presbyters, and whole church, come to a joint decision (Acts 15:22). They sent a joint letter, "It is the decision of the holy Spirit and of us, not to place on you any burden beyond these necessities . . ." (Acts 15:28). The *reception* is described: "when they read it, they rejoiced at the exhortation" (Acts 15:31).[25] This assembly exemplifies how "*a synodal church is a participatory and co-responsible church*": "*in a synodal style, decisions are made through discernment, based on a consensus that flows from the common obedience to the Spirit.*"[26] Fr. Radcliffe, the synod retreat preacher, hit upon this spirit of the synod when he declared:

> The bravest thing we can do in this synod is to be truthful about our doubts and questions with each other, the questions to which we have no clear answers. Then we shall draw near as fellow searchers, beggars for the truth . . . Friendship flourishes when we dare to share our doubts and seek the truth together.[27]

---

21. Okoye, "For a Synodal Church," 68.
22. Schönborn, "Lessons from the Council of Jerusalem" (italics original), §§19, 28.
23. Okoye, "For a Synodal Church," 68.
24. Schönborn, "Lessons from the Council of Jerusalem," §30.
25. Schönborn, "Lessons from the Council of Jerusalem," §31.
26. *PD*, 30. See Okoye, "For a Synodal Church," 69.
27. Radcliffe, "2 October 2023: First Meditation."

# 2

# Theological Footprints toward the Synod on Synodality

## VATICAN II (1962–65)

THE STANDARD IDEA OF the church in Vatican I (1869–70) and following it was institutional, *societas perfecta*[1] (perfect society); the dominant image was that of Mystical Body of Christ.[2] The church was divided into *ecclesia docens* (teaching church) and *ecclesia discerns* (learning church). Only the ordained have divinely authorized power to sanctify, teach, and rule. The power of the church is twofold—power of orders and power of jurisdiction.[3]

The self-understanding of the church shifted in Vatican II, "from the sociological to the biblical; from the jurisdictional to the sacramental; from the sectarian to the ecumenical; from the papal to the episcopal; from the hierarchical to the collegial."[4] The second draft (1963) of *Lumen gentium*

---

1. Chapter 10 of *Supremi pastoris* ends: "hence we must believe (*credenda*) that the church of Christ is a perfect society," that is, distinct from every other assembly of people, and moves towards its proper end by its own means (quoted in Granfield, "Church as *Societas Perfecta*").

2. Other images were *sponsa electa, sponsa Christi, gens sancta, populus acceptabilis, regnum Dei, civitas Dei* (chosen spouse, spouse of Christ, a holy nation, an acceptable people, kingdom of God, city of God).

3. Granfield, "Church as *Societas Perfecta*," 438.

4. Granfield, "Church as *Societas Perfecta*," 446.

(henceforth *LG*) still had chapter 2, "On the Hierarchical Constitution of the Church," precede chapter 3, "On the People of God and the Laity in Particular." The chapters were reversed in the intersession period, with tremendous results for ecclesiology.[5] "People of God" now meant all of Christ's faithful; it became the dominant paradigm of the church. Baptism stood out as the common dignity of all the faithful: "in the one Spirit we were all baptized into one body" (1 Cor 12:13). And "among all the baptized there is a genuine equality of dignity and a common responsibility for mission, according to the vocation of each."[6]

The obligation of spreading the faith is imposed on every disciple of Christ according to his ability (*LG*, 17)—this not by delegation, but by virtue of baptism and confirmation. For the first time in a council of the church, *LG*, 10 spoke in detail of the common priesthood of the faithful as a participation in the priesthood of Christ (though differing in essence, not only in degree, from the ministerial priesthood). *Ad gentes, Decree on the Missionary Activity of the Church* (henceforth *AG*), the most theologically consistent document of the Council, rooted the church and its mission in the Trinity: "The pilgrim church is missionary by her very nature. For it is from the mission of the Son and the mission of the Holy Spirit that she takes her origin, in accordance with the decree of God the Father" (*AG*, 2). Hence, "sharing [God's] mission is indeed constitutive of the church, which, like the Trinity, is a communion-in-*mission*."[7]

Vatican II did not develop a theology of communion (*koinōnia*) or explore all of its practical implications,[8] but it furnished the building blocks for such theology. The word *communion* appears with different dimensions and applications in the documents of the Council. The concept is also conveyed through other words, like *unio* (used synonymously with *communio*).[9] "So in the conciliar documents we have to do with a *concept which is only in the process of development*."[10] Nevertheless, in *LG*, 1, the church is designated as a kind of sacrament or sign and instrument of intimate union with God and of the unity of all humankind (*intimae cum Deo unionis totiusque generis humani unitatis*). In the *Decree on Ecumenism*

---

5. Philips, "Lumen gentium," 110; Rush, *Vision of Vatican II*, 289.
6. Synod of Bishops, *Synthesis Report*, ch. 3, c.
7. Bevans, "Revising Mission at Vatican II," 276.
8. Lennan, "Communion Ecclesiology," 25.
9. Rush, *Vision of Vatican II*, 203, 205.
10. Kasper, *Theology and Church*, 151 (italics original).

(*Unitatis redintegratio*, henceforth *UR*) no. 2, the Trinity of Persons of one God, the Father and the Son in the Holy Spirit, is the highest exemplar and source of the mystery of the unity of the church. This means that "the call to *communio* is based on the *communio* between the divine persons in the Trinity."[11] Because each particular church, gathered around its bishop, is the church of Jesus Christ, "the Eucharist is therefore the highpoint of Christian communion."[12] The individual bishop represents his own church, but all of them together, in union with the pope, represent the entire Church joined in the bond of peace, love, and unity.[13] For, "in and from such individual churches there comes into being the one and only Catholic church" (*LG*, 23). The Council found it opportune that bishops belonging to the same nation or region form an association and meet together "at fixed times . . . in the service of the common good of the churches" (*CD*, 37). The phrase *communio ecclesiarum* ("communion of churches") occurs twice in the Vatican documents, in *AG* 19 and 38. Promulgated on the second-to-last working day of the Council, this document draws on and develops the riches of the other documents and is one of the richest ecclesiological texts of the council.[14] *AG*, 19 says: "Let the young churches preserve an intimate communion with the church universal" (*Intima permaneat ecclesiarum novellarum communio cum tota Ecclesia*). *AG*, 38: "From this fact [that bishops are consecrated not just for some one diocese, but for the salvation of the entire world] arises that communion and cooperation [*illa communio et cooperatio Ecclesiarum*] between churches which is so necessary today for carrying on the work of evangelization." There is *communio hierarchica* of bishops with and under the pope: "A person becomes a *member of the College* by virtue of episcopal consecration and hierarchical communion with the head of the College and its members."[15] Kasper argues that "the communion of the churches and the collegiality of the bishops is based on the more fundamental communion [communion of the faithful] which is

---

11. Rush, *Vision of Vatican II*, 204.

12. Kasper, "Church as Communion," 236.

13. In governing their own particular churches well, bishops effectively contribute to the welfare of the whole Mystical Body, which is also the body of the churches (*quod est etiam corpus Ecclesiarum*).

14. Rush, *Vision of Vatican II*, 209–10.

15. "Prefatory Note of Explanation" attached to the end of ch. 3 of *LG* (italics original), announced by the Secretary General of the Council at the 123rd General Congregation, Nov 16, 1964, not voted on by the Council, but said to come from "a higher authority."

the church, the People of God itself."[16] Others see these two as interrelated and interdependent.[17]

The reception of Vatican II was marked by debate on its interpretation. There were tensions in the Council documents deriving from the occasional juxtaposition of traditional and newer ideas. Also, new passages were sometimes inserted into paragraphs already voted on, but which had been formulated according to a different mindset.[18] Because of this, "Vatican II presents its receivers with a task of synthesizing the elements of its vision, something that it itself was unable to achieve or was not even intending to do."[19] Gaillardetz also points out the tension between two ecclesiological approaches,[20] leading to the dispute between Cardinal Ratzinger and Cardinal Kasper[21] that ended in a rapprochement.[22]

## THE RATZINGER REPORT

Cardinal Ratzinger gave an interview to Vittorio Messori in August 1984.[23] He called for "restoration," by which he meant "the search for a new balance after all the exaggerations of an indiscriminate opening to the world, after the overly positive interpretations of an agnostic and atheistic world."[24] When the press pounced on the word *restoration*, he explained that semantically it means a recovery of lost values, within a new totality.[25] Was there rupture or continuity? There is not "a 'break' and an abandonment of the

---

16. Kasper, *Theology and Church*, 161.
17. On this see Rush, *Vision of Vatican II*, 214–15.
18. Rush, *Vision of Vatican II*, 193.
19. Rush, *Vision of Vatican II*, 335.
20. Gaillardetz, *Ecclesiology for a Global Church*, 109. "One begins with the local church and sees the universal church as a communion of local churches, and the other maintains a pre-conciliar universality that privileges the universal church."
21. McDonnell, "Ratzinger/Kasper Debate," 227–50; Kasper, "Friendly Reply to Cardinal Ratzinger," 8–14; Ratzinger, "Response to Walter Kasper," 7–11.
22. See Gaillardetz, *Ecclesiology for a Global Church*, 118. Kasper agreed that the mystery of the church is preexistent, yet this does not mean the priority of the universal church since this mystery includes both the universal and local dimensions of the church's eventual historical reality, and Ratzinger insisted that universal church has priority, but this does not contradict the simultaneity of the universal and local church in history.
23. Published in English as *Ratzinger Report*. Translated from the German.
24. Messori, *Ratzinger Report*, 37.
25. Messori, *Ratzinger Report*, 38n5.

tradition. There is, instead, a continuity that allows neither a return to the past nor a flight forward."[26] The documents of Vatican II must be read in continuity with those of Vatican 1 and Trent[27]: "It is impossible (for a Catholic) to take a position for or against Trent or Vatican I . . . . It is likewise impossible to decide in favor of Trent and Vatican I, but against Vatican II. Whoever denies Vatican II denies the authority that upholds the other two councils."[28] He pleaded "to return to the authentic texts of the original Vatican II,"[29] convinced that "its [Vatican II's] authentic reception has not yet begun: its documents were quickly buried under a pile of superficial or frankly inexact publications. The reading of the *letter* of the documents will enable us to discover their true *spirit*."[30]

> Episcopal conferences have no theological basis, they do not belong to the structure of the Church, as willed by Christ . . . they have only practical, concrete function . . . . No episcopal conference, as such, has a teaching mission; its documents have no weight of their own save that of the consent given to them by the individual bishops . . .[31] [he insists on this because] it is a matter of safeguarding the very nature of the Catholic Church, which is based on an episcopal structure and not on a kind of federation of national churches. The national level is not an ecclesial dimension.[32]

## THE EXTRAORDINARY SYNOD OF BISHOPS, NOVEMBER 24–DECEMBER 8, 1985

The same year *The Ratzinger Report* was published, John Paul II convoked the Second Extraordinary General Assembly with the topic "The Twentieth Anniversary of the Conclusion of the Second Vatican Council." Only the presidents of episcopal conferences were invited. The question on many

---

26. Messori, *Ratzinger Report*, 31.
27. See Hughes, "Review of *Ratzinger Report*," 312.
28. Messori, *Ratzinger Report*, 28.
29. Messori, *Ratzinger Report*, 31.
30. Messori, *Ratzinger Report*, 40 (italics original).
31. He refers to the 1983 Code, canon 455.4 and 1, which prescribes that episcopal conferences cannot validly act "in the name of all the bishops unless each and every bishop has given his consent," except where the common law prescribes it or a special mandate of the Apostolic See determines it.
32. Messori, *Ratzinger Report*, 59–60.

minds was this: "was 'restoration' in his [Ratzinger's] sense going to be the agenda of the synod?"[33] It turned out that Cardinal Walter Kasper had a major role in this synod and its procedure. Kasper himself wrote:

> While studying the council documents in preparation for my work, I came to the conclusion that *communio*-ecclesiology was the central concern and the main motif of the conciliar ecclesiology. Together with the relator of the Synod, Cardinal Godfried Daneels von Meecheln, I was able to contribute this aspect to the Synod. It has become fundamental for me ever since.[34]

The synod was given the right to prepare its own Final Report. It found that beside valid interpretations of the Council there had been deficiencies and difficulties, hence the need for a deeper reception of the Council (I, 2). The four major Constitutions should serve as interpretive key to the whole documents of the Council. The various descriptions of the church—People of God, Body of Christ, Bride of Christ, Temple of the Holy Spirit, Family of God—complete one another, but communion/*koinōnia*[35] provides the right context for these terms (IIa, 2). Hence, "the ecclesiology of communion is the central and fundamental idea of the Council's documents" (IIc.1). Communion is above all with the living God, Father, Son, and Holy Spirit. The church is "a people made one with the unity of the Father, the Son, and the Holy Spirit" (*LG*, 4; St. Cyprian, *De oratione dominica*, 23; Augustine, *Sermo*, 71, 20, 33). Trinitarian communion should be reflected in the structures and internal relations of the church. The ecclesiology of communion provides the sacramental foundation of collegiality (IIc.4) of the pope alone and the pope with the bishops, the College never being without its head (*LG*, 22). Partial realizations are the Synod of Bishops, Episcopal Conferences, the Roman Curia, and *Ad Limina* visits. "The inalienable responsibility of each bishop in relation to the church, particular and universal, calls for deeper study of the theological and juridical status of episcopal conferences, especially the issue of their doctrinal authority" (IIc, 5).[36] The message of Vatican II remains the "Magna Carta" for the future (7c).

---

33. O'Riordan, "Synod of Bishops 1985," 141.

34. Kasper, *Catholic Church*, 21.

35. *Communio* translates the Greek *koinōnia* which originally did not mean "community" but "participation." See Hauck, "*Koinos*," 3:789–97; in the New Testament, especially in the good of salvation granted by God.

36. This in light of *CD*, 38, and canons 447 and 753 of the 1983 Code.

After the 1985 Extraordinary Synod, the theology of communion became *the* interpretive key for the council's ecclesiology. The ecclesiology of communion opened the path toward the synod on synodality.

Two views of communion, expressed already in that synod, continued to clash. One view was that of institutional unity focused on discipline and obedience as the grounds of communion. The other was participative, authority listening more to the people and taking into account their insights and feelings.[37] Comblin feared that the communion model restricts the richer theology of the church as People of God by emphasizing vertical relations and authority rather than reciprocity.[38] It lacks the capacity to generate preferential option for the poor. Clare Watkins was concerned that the resonance of "communion" will erase the urgency of the call to mission.[39] Kasper continued writing on communion, especially as concerns ecumenism.[40] A *federalist* type of communion views the church as a whole coming to being through the mutual acknowledgment and acceptance of the local churches, in contrast to *LG* in which the universal exists within each local church. A *centralist* view sees the local church as a mere secondary manifestation of the church as a whole, in contrast to the view of the local church around its bishop as the real church of Christ in one particular place, not as an administrative district of the church. There is also the Anglican proposal of the communial unity of each local church with Peter and under Peter, though member churches would lose nothing of their essential reality as churches if this was lacking.[41]

## CONGREGATION FOR DOCTRINE OF THE FAITH (CDF), SOME ASPECTS OF THE CHURCH UNDERSTOOD AS COMMUNION, MAY 28, 1992

Aligning with the teaching of the Extraordinary Synod, the CDF affirmed that "the concept of *communion* lies '*at the heart of the Church's self-understanding*'" (no. 3).[42] Because "the universal church becomes present in them [particular churches] with all its essential elements," one understands

37. O'Riordan, "Synod of Bishops 1985," 150.
38. Comblin, *People of God*, 56–58.
39. Watkins, "Objecting to Koinonia," 341.
40. Kasper, *Theology and Church*, 148–65; Kasper, "Church as Communion," 232–44.
41. See Kasper, "Church as Communion," 239–43.
42. John Paul II, "Address to Bishops of the USA."

the universal church as a "communion of churches." Against the Anglican position on ecumenism above, it affirms that "the universal church cannot be conceived as the sum of the particular churches, or as a federation of particular churches" (no. 9).[43] The ministry of Peter belongs already to the essence of each particular church from within (no. 13).[44] There is thus a relation of "mutual interiority" between universal and particular church (no. 9) such that, "*the Church in and formed out of the Churches* (*ecclesia in et ex ecclesiis*) [LG 23a] is inseparable from this other formula, *The Churches in and formed out of the Church* (*ecclesia in et ex Ecclesiis*)" (no. 9).[45] It is not the result of the communion of the churches, but, in its essential mystery, it is a reality *ontologically and temporally* prior to every *individual* particular Church (no. 9).

## POPE FRANCIS, *EVANGELII GAUDIUM*, *THE JOY OF THE GOSPEL*, NOVEMBER 24, 2013

Pope Francis's first encyclical, *Evangelii gaudium*, can be shown to have laid out the scaffolding of themes later taken up by the synod on synodality. His ultimate concern was "the reform of the church in her missionary outreach" (no. 17a), an ecclesial renewal which cannot be deferred (no. 27). He dreamed of a "missionary option," that is, a missionary impulse capable of transforming everything, so that the church's customs, ways of doing things, times and schedules, language and structures can be suitably channeled for the evangelization of today's world rather than for her self-preservation (no. 27).[46]

> The Gospel joy which enlivens the community of disciples is a missionary joy (no. 21). [He longs for] a church which goes forth . . . where "Jesus' command to 'go and make disciples' echoes . . . and all of us are called to take part in this new missionary 'going forth'" (nos. 19, 20). The entire People of God proclaims the Gospel (no. 110). Evangelization is the task of the church . . . she is first and foremost a people advancing on its pilgrim way towards God (no. 111).

---

43. See John Paul II, "Address to the Roman Curia."
44. John Paul II, "Address to Bishops of the USA," no. 4.
45. John Paul II, "Address to Roman Curia," no. 9.
46. This can be seen as a summary of what synodality is about.

> *We are all missionary disciples.* In virtue of baptism, all the members of the People of God have become missionary disciples (cf. Matt 28:19).... Every Christian is a missionary to the extent that he or she has encountered the love of God in Christ Jesus (no. 120). All of us are called to offer others an explicit witness to the saving love of the Lord (no. 121).

Baptism "is at the root of the principle of synodality."[47]

In all its activities the parish encourages and trains its members to be evangelizers.[48] "It is a . . . center of constant missionary outreach" (no. 28). "Each particular church . . . is likewise called to missionary conversion" (no. 30). Pastoral ministry in a missionary key seeks to abandon the complacent attitude that says, "We have always done it this way." The pope invited everyone to be bold and creative in this task of rethinking the goals, structures, style, and methods of evangelization in their respective communities (no. 33).

Science is not opposed to faith.[49] "Dialogue between science and faith also belongs to the work of evangelization at the service of peace."[50]

> Faith is not fearful of reason; on the contrary, it seeks and trusts reason, since "the light of reason and the light of faith both come from God" [Aquinas, *Summa contra Gentiles*, 14] and cannot contradict each other (no. 242).

"There are ecclesial structures which can hamper efforts at evangelization, yet even good structures are only helpful when there is a life constantly driving, sustaining, and assessing them" (no. 26).

"Nor do I believe that the papal magisterium should be expected to offer a definitive or complete word on every question which affects the church and the world. It is not advisable for the Pope to take the place of the local Bishops in the discernment of every issue which arises in their territory." In this sense, he declares himself conscious of the need to promote a sound "decentralization" (no. 16). "A juridical status of episcopal conferences would see them as subjects of specific attributions, including genuine doctrinal authority. Excessive centralization, rather than proving helpful, complicates the church's life and her missionary outreach" (no. 32).

---

47. Synod of Bishops, *Synthesis Report*, ch. 7, b.
48. John Paul II, *CL*, Propositio 44.
49. This will be debated at the synod on synodality.
50. John Paul II, *CL*, Propositio 54.

This seems to counter Ratzinger's earlier affirmation that "episcopal conferences have no theological basis, they do not belong to the structure of the church, as willed by Christ."[51] For Francis, "the missionary key" is the measure of the church's being and activity.

## INTERNATIONAL THEOLOGICAL COMMISSION, *SENSUS FIDEI* IN THE LIFE OF THE CHURCH, 2014

The Commission began work on this document in 2009 but finished it in 2014, a year after the installation of Pope Francis. It became one of the theological underpinnings of synodality.

All the baptized receive from the Holy Spirit an anointing that teaches them (1 John 2:20, 27; John 16:13). Hence,

> the faithful have an instinct for the truth of the Gospel, which enables them to recognize and endorse authentic Christian doctrine and practice, and to reject what is false (no. 2).... the virtue of faith establishes a connaturality between the believing subject and the authentic object of faith (no. 50). [As such,] "the whole body of the faithful ... cannot err in matters of belief" (*LG*, 12). The "Spirit of truth" arouses and sustains in them a "supernatural appreciation of the faith" (*supernaturali sensu fidei*), shown when the whole people, from the bishops to the last of the faithful ... manifest a universal consent in matters of faith and morals (no. 44). This *sensus fidei*, though infallible in itself with regard to its object (no. 55), develops in proportion to the development of the virtue of faith ... and is therefore proportional to the holiness of one's life (no. 57). It is not to be identified with "the opinion of a large number of Christians" (no. 47) or "public or majority opinion" (no. 118), rather is a property of theological faith. The *consensus fidelium* constitutes a sure criterion for recognizing a particular teaching or practice as in accord with the apostolic Tradition (no. 66).

On those occasions when magisterial teaching meets with difficulty or resistance on the part of the faithful, the faithful must reflect again on the teaching, while the magisterium considers whether it needs clarification or reformulation (no. 80).

---

51. Messori, *Ratzinger Report*, 59–60. This view is enshrined in the 1983 Code of Canon Law, canons 447–459.

## POPE FRANCIS, ADDRESS AT CEREMONY COMMEMORATING THE 50TH ANNIVERSARY OF THE SYNOD OF BISHOPS, OCTOBER 17, 2015

The pope declared, "It is precisely this path of *synodality* which God expects of the church of the third millennium." He recalled *LG*, 12 which says that the whole body of the faithful cannot err in matters of belief, being *infallibile in credendo* ("infallible in believing").

> The *sensus fidei* prevents a rigid separation between an *ecclesia docens* [teaching church] and an *ecclesia discens* [learning church] since the flock likewise has an instinctive ability to discern the new ways that the Lord is revealing to the church.... A synodal church is a church which listens ... a mutual listening in which everyone has something to learn. The faithful people, the College of Bishops, the Bishop of Rome: all listening to each other, and all listening to the Holy Spirit, the "Spirit of truth" (John 14:17), in order to know what he "says to the churches."
>
> If we understand, as Saint John Chrysostom says, that "Church and Synod are synonymous,"[52] then, *synodality* [italics original], as a constitutive element of the church, offers us the most appropriate interpretive framework for understanding the hierarchical ministry itself.... In [Christ's] church, as in an inverted pyramid, the top is located beneath the base. Consequently, those who exercise authority are called "ministers," because, in the original meaning of the word, they are the least of all. It is in serving the People of God that each bishop becomes, for that portion of the flock entrusted to him, *vicarius Christi*, the vicar of that Jesus who at the Last Supper bent down to wash the feet of the Apostles (cf. John 13:1–15). For disciples of Jesus, yesterday, today, and always, the only authority is the authority of service, the only power is the power of the cross.

Pope Francis used the occasion to articulate the underlying theology and spirituality of synodality. The phrases "synodality," "a constitutive element of the church," and "an inverted pyramid" will echo throughout the synod documents and the synodal discussions.

---

52. Chrysostom, *Explicatio in Ps 149: PG* 55, 493.

## INTERNATIONAL THEOLOGICAL COMMISSION, SYNODALITY IN THE LIFE AND MISSION OF THE CHURCH, MARCH 2, 2018

Synodality operates on "the ecclesiology of the People of God" (no. 6). The Church of Christ being "an ecclesiological *perichoresis* in which trinitarian communion sees its ecclesial reflection" (no. 60), "a synodal church is a church of participation and co-responsibility" (no. 67). "Synodality is lived out in the church in the service of mission. *Ecclesia peregrinans natura sua missionaria* ['the pilgrim church is by its very nature missionary,' AG, 2]. She exists in order to evangelize" (no. 53; EN, 14). "All members of the church are agents of evangelization" (no. 9; EG, 120).

> The anointing of the Holy Spirit is manifested in the *sensus fidei* of the faithful . . . the presence of the Spirit gives Christians a certain connaturality with divine realities (no. 56; EG, 119). This gift of the Holy Spirit . . . is manifested in the equal dignity of the baptized; the universal call to holiness; the participation of all the faithful in the priestly, prophetic, and royal office of Jesus Christ; the richness of hierarchical and charismatic gifts; the life and mission of each local church (no. 46). . . . Personal conversion to the spirituality of communion [calls] for transition from "I" understood in a self-centered way to the ecclesial "we," where every "I," clothed in Christ, . . . journeys together with their brothers and sisters.

Hence the church becomes "the home and school of communion"[53] (no. 107).

Synodality calls for "*structures* and *ecclesial processes* in which the synodal nature of the church is expressed at an institutional level, but analogously on various levels" (no. 70b; italics original).

> In the Catholic and apostolic vision of synodality there is a reciprocal relationship between the *communio fidelium* (communion of the faithful), the *communio episcoporum* (communion of bishops), and the *communio ecclesiarum* (communion of churches). The concept of synodality is broader than that of collegiality because it includes the participation of all in the church and that of all the churches (no. 66).

"The first level on which synodality is exercised is the local church" (77). Within the local church, exercises of synodality are: "the Diocesan Curia, the College of Consultors, the Chapter of Canons and the Financial

---

53. John Paul II, *Novo Millennio Ineunte*, nos. 43, 197.

Council" (no. 80). Vatican II stipulated that the Council of Priests and the Diocesan Pastoral Council (*CD*, 27) be set up as permanent bodies for the exercise and promotion of communion and synodality. "The Diocesan Pastoral Council is proposed as the most appropriate permanent structure for implementing synodality in the local church" (no. 81). At the parish level, synodal structures are the parish pastoral council and the financial council.

"Individual bishops represent each his own church," while the College of Bishops, with the Pope at its head, represents the entire church (*LG*, 23). Thus, "an Ecumenical Council is the supreme instance of ecclesial synodality in the communion of the Bishops with the Pope" (no. 98).

> Regional synodal structures in the Latin-rite Catholic Church include: Provincial and General Councils, Episcopal Conferences and groupings of Episcopal Conferences, sometimes at a continental level; in the Eastern-rite Catholic Church: the Patriarchal and Provincial Synods, the Assembly of Hierarchs of various eastern Churches *sui iuris*, and the Council of Eastern Catholic Patriarchs (no. 87).

"The College of Cardinals, originally composed of the Priests and Deacons of the Church of Rome and the Bishops of the suburbicarian dioceses, is the historical synodal Council of the Bishop of Rome" (no. 101).

"The Roman Curia is a permanent service to the Pope's ministry in favor of the universal church which, by its nature, is intimately related to episcopal collegiality and ecclesial synodality" (no. 102). The Synod of Bishops was instituted by St. Paul VI in 1965 "as a permanent synodal structure" (no. 99).

The past history of relationships in the church may point forward to possible new structures of synodality. O'Malley writes:

> In the first millennium popes did not "run the church," nor did they claim to. They defined no doctrines; they wrote no encyclicals; they called no bishops *ad limina*. They did not convoke ecumenical councils, and they did not preside at them. In fact, their roles in the first eight councils were generally insignificant. In the early Middle Ages (and well beyond) the popes' principal duty, many believed, was to guard the tombs of the apostles and officiate at the solemn liturgies at the great basilicas. In that period, although some of the popes of course had a broad vision of their responsibilities and dealt about weighty matters with the leaders of society, for the most part they behaved as essentially local figures, intent on local issues.[54]

---

54. O'Malley, "Millennium and the Papalization," 11; cited in Rush, *Vision of Vatican II*, 285n5.

# 3

# Canonical Footprints toward the Synod on Synodality

### JOHN PAUL II, MOTU PROPRIO *APOSTOLOS SUOS*, ON THE THEOLOGICAL AND JURIDICAL NATURE OF EPISCOPAL CONFERENCES, MAY 21, 1998

AS MENTIONED ABOVE, THE 1985 Extraordinary Synod called for a fuller and more profound study of the theological and, consequently, the juridical status of episcopal conferences, and above all of the issue of their doctrinal authority, in the light of no. 38 of the conciliar decree *Christus Dominus* and canons 447 and 753[1] of the Code of Canon Law[2] (no. 7). The Motu Proprio *Apostolos suos* answered that call, reaffirming canon 455.4. "The competence of individual diocesan bishops remains intact; and neither the conference[3] nor its president may act in the name of all the bishops unless

---

1. "Whether they teach individually, or in episcopal conferences, or gathered together in particular councils, bishops in communion with the head and the members of the College, while not infallible in their teaching, are the authentic instructors and teachers of the faith for Christ's faithful entrusted to their care. The faithful are bound to adhere, with a religious submission of mind, to this authentic *magisterium* of their bishops."

2. Episcopal conference as assembly of bishops "exercising together certain pastoral offices for Christ's faithful of that territory."

3. No. 15 of this Motu Proprio helpfully outlines issues which episcopal conferences handle: "the promotion and safeguarding of faith and morals, the translation of liturgical

each and every bishop has given his consent" (no. 20). The conference may not hinder the authority of the individual bishop nor substitute itself for it (no. 24).

Some areas of doctrinal competence may be seeing "that catechisms are issued for its own territory if such seems useful, with the prior approval of the Apostolic See" (canon 775.2) and approving editions of the books of Sacred Scripture and their translations (canon 825). A doctrinal declaration of an episcopal conference, if approved unanimously, may be issued in the name of that conference only; if unanimity is lacking, "a majority alone of the bishops of a conference cannot issue a declaration as authentic teaching of the conference to which all the faithful of the territory would have to adhere, unless it obtains the *recognitio* of the Apostolic See, which will not give it if the majority requesting it is not substantial" (no. 22).

> In order that the doctrinal declarations of the conference of bishops referred to in no. 22 of the present Letter may constitute authentic magisterium and be published in the name of the conference itself, they must be unanimously approved by the bishops who are members, or receive the *recognitio* of the Apostolic See if approved in plenary assembly by at least two thirds of the bishops belonging to the conference and having a deliberative vote (Art. 1).

## POPE BENEDICT XVI, MOTU PROPRIO, *OMNIUM IN MENTEM* ON SEVERAL AMENDMENTS TO THE CODE OF CANON LAW, OCTOBER 26, 2009

Canons 1008 and 1009 (on the sacrament of Holy Orders) reaffirm "the essential distinction between the common priesthood of the faithful and the ministerial priesthood," while distinguishing the episcopate, the presbyterate, and the diaconate. Pope John Paul II, "after consulting the Fathers of the Congregation for the Doctrine of the Faith, on October 9, 1998, ordered that the text of no. 1581 of the *Catechism of the Catholic Church* be modified in order better to convey the teaching on deacons" found in *LG*, 29. Benedict XVI adjusted the canon on the matter accordingly.

---

books, the promotion and formation of priestly vocations, the preparation of catechetical aids, the promotion and safeguarding of Catholic universities and other educational centers, the ecumenical task, relations with civil authorities, the defense of human life, of peace, and of human rights, also in order to ensure their protection in civil legislation, the promotion of social justice, the use of the means of social communication, etc."

The changes ordered by John Paul II to the second sentence of *Catechism* no. 1581 do not reflect in the English editions (1994, 1998), nor even in the text at the Vatican web site, but in the *editio typica*.[4]

> *Catechism*, no. 1581:
>
> By ordination one is enabled to act as a representative of Christ, Head of the Church, in his triple office of priest, prophet, and king.
>
> *Per ordinationem recipitur capacitas agendi tamquam Christi legatus, Capitis Ecclesiae, in eius triplici munere sacerdotis, prophetae et regis.*
>
> *Editio typica*:
>
> From him [Christ] bishops and priests receive the mission and capacity to act in the person of Christ the Head, deacons however the power to serve the People of God in the service of the liturgy, the word, and of charity [my translation].
>
> *Ab eo (sc. Christo) Episcopi et presbyteri missionem et facultatem agendi in persona Christi Capitis accipiunt, diaconi vero vim populo Dei serviendi in "diaconia" liturgiae, verbi et caritatis.*

Canon 1008 before the change read:

> By divine institution, the sacrament of orders establishes some among the Christian faithful as sacred ministers through an indelible character which marks them. They are consecrated and designated, each according to his grade, to nourish the people of God, fulfilling in the person of Christ the Head the functions of teaching, sanctifying, and governing.[5]

Canon 1008 now reads (italics indicate the changes):

> By divine institution, some of the Christian faithful are marked with an indelible character and *constituted* as sacred ministers by the sacrament of *holy* orders. They are thus consecrated and *deputed* so that, each according to his own grade, they may serve the People of God by *a new and specific title*.[6]

Canon 1009 is given a new third paragraph, as follows:

---

4. Text of the change in Latin from Coccopalmerio, "On Omnium in Mentem."

5. This seems to make deacons (as well as priests and bishops) act in the person of Christ the Head.

6. Omitted: "fulfilling in the person of Christ the Head the functions of teaching, sanctifying, and governing."

> Those who are constituted in the order of the episcopate or the presbyterate receive the mission and capacity to act in the person of Christ the Head, whereas deacons are empowered to serve the People of God in the ministries of the liturgy, the word and charity.

The diaconate is distinguished from the other two Orders; the deacon does not act "in the person of Christ the Head" (Art. 2). This will gain importance in the synod's discussion of the nature of the diaconate, and particularly the possibility of women deacons.

## POPE FRANCIS, *MAGNUM PRINCIPIUM*, SEPTEMBER 3, 2017

The Motu Proprio *Magnum principium* of September 3, 2017, modified canon 838 of the 1983 Code concerning vernacular translations of the liturgy. The canon now reads as follows (italics denoting the papal modifications):

> It pertains to the episcopal conferences to *faithfully* prepare versions of the liturgical books in vernacular languages, suitably *accommodated* within defined limits, and *to approve and publish the liturgical books for the regions for which they are responsible after the confirmation of the Apostolic See.*

The episcopal conference prepares and *approves* the version, the Congregation for Divine Worship and the Discipline of the Sacraments *ratifies* the approval of the bishops. Cardinal Sarah, then prefect of that Congregation, had publicly and strongly opposed this. The pope clarified the ratification as "recogniz[ing] adaptations approved by the episcopal conference according to the norm of law"; this includes "the more radical adaptations established and approved by episcopal conferences." Pope Francis believes that the episcopal conference is more competent to judge prayers in the mother tongue, while the Apostolic See oversees the areas of unity and fidelity to the tradition.

## POPE FRANCIS, APOSTOLIC CONSTITUTION *EPISCOPALIS COMMUNIO*, ON THE SYNOD OF BISHOPS, SEPTEMBER 15, 2018

Paul VI instituted the Synod of Bishops with his Motu Proprio *Apostolica sollicitudo* promulgated on September 15, 1965. With his *Ordo Synodi*

*Episcoporum* of September 29, 2006, and the attached *Adnexum de modo procedendi in circulis minoribus*, Benedict XVI revised the norms for the Synod of Bishops. The present Apostolic Constitution replaces both documents.

Synod assemblies have "served as a privileged locus of interpretation and reception of the rich conciliar magisterium, but they have also given a significant impetus to subsequent papal magisterium" (no. 1). The synod has consultative vote; however, the pope notes that the vote of the synod fathers, "if morally unanimous, has a qualitative ecclesial weight which surpasses the merely formal aspect of the consultative vote."[7] The synod "might enjoy deliberative power, should the Roman Pontiff wish to grant this" (no. 3; *CD*, no. 5; canon 337.3).

Following a procedure that he already adopted for the synod on the family, the pope legislated that "if circumstances so suggest, a single synodal assembly may be spread over more than one session" (no. 8; Art. 3.1). To the members of the synod listed in canon 346 (only bishops and some members of clerical religious institutes—"clerical" excludes women religious), he legislated that "according to the theme and the circumstances, certain others who are not bishops may be summoned to the synod assembly; their role is determined in each case by the Roman Pontiff" (Art. 2.2). This leaves open the nomination of non-bishops as members, with vote.

"The General Secretary and the Undersecretary are appointed by the Roman Pontiff and are members of the synod assembly" (Art. 22.3). This means that even if these are non-bishops they would still have the vote. Article 7.2 notes that the right of the faithful, individually or in association with others, to submit their contributions directly to the General Secretariat of the Synod, remains intact.

The Final Document, if "expressly approved by the Roman Pontiff,"

> participates in the ordinary magisterium of the Successor of Peter (Art. 18.1). If the Roman Pontiff has granted deliberative power to the synod assembly, according to the norm of canon 343 of the Code of Canon Law, the Final Document participates in the ordinary magisterium of the Successor of Peter once it has been ratified and promulgated by him (Art. 18.2). In this case, the Final Document is published with the signature of the Roman Pontiff together with that of the members.

---

7. John Paul II, "Theological Basis."

On April 26, 2023, the Synod Secretariat announced that Pope Francis modified this Constitution somewhat by adding non-bishops as voting members, though less than 25 percent of the membership. However, this did not change the nature of the assembly as synod of bishops.

## CONGREGATION FOR CLERGY, INSTRUCTION, THE PASTORAL CONVERSION OF THE PARISH COMMUNITY IN THE SERVICE OF THE EVANGELIZING MISSION OF THE CHURCH, JULY 20, 2020

> The subject of the missionary and evangelizing action of the church is always the People of God as a whole.... the parish is not identified as a building or a series of structures, but rather as a specific community of the faithful, where the parish priest is the proper pastor (no. 27; canons 515; 518; 519). [Seeing that] the Lord taught his disciples to have a generous spirit of service ... and to have a special care for the poor, the need arises not to "commercialise" the sacramental life, and not to give the impression that the celebration of the sacraments, especially the Holy Eucharist, along with other ministerial activities, are subject to tariffs (no. 40).

The office of parish priest, or pastor, "involves the full care of souls" and belongs only to those ordained as presbyter, thus excluding the possibility of conferring this office (*parochus*) on one who lacks this Order, "even where priests are scarce." Nor may it be entrusted to a juridic person or "a group composed of clerics and lay people. Consequently, appellations such as 'team leader,' 'équipe leader,' or the like, which convey a sense of collegial government of the parish, are to be avoided" (no. 66). However, in "pastorally problematic circumstances,[8] in order to sustain Christian life and to continue the evangelizing mission of the community, the diocesan bishop may entrust the pastoral care of a parish to a deacon, a consecrated religious or layperson, or even a group of persons (e.g., Religious Institute, Association)" (no. 87; canon 157.2). These take care "to perform only those functions that correspond to their respective status as deacons or lay

---

8. These are strictly laid out in no. 89: "(a) *ob sacerdotum penuriam* and not for reasons of convenience or ambiguous 'advancement of the laity'; (b) this is *participatio in exercitio curae pastoralis* and not directing, coordinating, moderating or governing the parish; these competencies, according to the canon, are the competencies of a priest alone."

faithful" (no. 92); they are directed by a priest with faculties who acts as "moderator of pastoral care."

> Care must be taken not to designate laity or religious as "pastor," "co-pastor," "chaplain," "moderator," "coordinator," "parish manager," or other similar terms reserved by law to priests. . . . it is likewise illegitimate, and not in conformity with their vocational identity, to use expressions such as "entrust the pastoral care of a parish," "preside over the parish community," and other similar phrases, that pertain to the distinct sacerdotal ministry of a parish priest (no. 96).

More appropriate would be terms like "Deacon Cooperator" or "Coordinator of (a particular sector of pastoral care)," "Pastoral Cooperator" or "Pastoral Associate or Assistant." In other words, pastoral care of the faithful is proper to priests.

> The lay faithful may preach in a church or oratory, if circumstances, necessity, or a particular case calls for it, "according to the prescripts of the episcopal conference" and "when expressly permitted by law or liturgical norms, as long as conditions contained in them are observed." However, [they] may not in any case give the homily during the celebration of the Eucharist (no. 99; canon 767 §1). Where there is a lack of priests and deacons, the diocesan bishop can delegate lay persons to assist at marriages (no. 100).

## POPE FRANCIS, CEAMA AS PUBLIC JURIDICAL PERSON, OCTOBER 9, 2020

CEAMA, the Ecclesial Conference of the Amazon, was established in June 2020 to promote synodality among the region's churches following the Amazon Synod of 2019.[9] Its creation was proposed in that synod's Final Document. The pope has now set it up as a "public juridical person." The nine countries involved are Brazil, Bolivia, Columbia, Ecuador, Peru, Venezuela, Suriname, Guiana, and French Guiana. What is particular in this is the broad participation, with bishops, of the lay faithful in a *pastoral de conjuncto*.

---

9. Zengarini, "Joy for the Creation."

## POPE FRANCIS, MOTU PROPRIO, *TRADITIONIS CUSTODES*, ON THE USE OF THE ROMAN LITURGY PRIOR TO THE REFORM OF 1970, JULY 16, 2021

Pope Francis issued this document after consultation of the world's bishops. It abrogates directives in this matter given by Saint John Paul II and Benedict XVI,[10] intended "to facilitate the ecclesial communion of those Catholics who feel attached to some earlier liturgical forms."

Article 1 legislates that "the liturgical books promulgated by Saint Paul VI and Saint John Paul II, in conformity with the decrees of Vatican Council II, are the unique expression of the *lex orandi* of the Roman Rite." "Unique expression" seems to rule out any idea of an "Extraordinary Order of Mass." Bishops having groups hitherto celebrating according to the 1962 Missal are, "to designate one or more locations where the faithful adherents of these groups may gather for the eucharistic celebration (not however in the parochial churches and without the erection of new personal parishes; Art. 3.2). They are, however, "to take care not to authorize the establishment of new groups" (3.6). Besides, "Priests ordained after the publication of the present Motu Proprio, who wish to celebrate using the *Missale Romanum* of 1962, should submit a formal request to the diocesan bishop who shall consult the Apostolic See before granting this authorization" (Art. 4).

## POPE FRANCIS: THE APOSTOLIC CONSTITUTION *PRAEDICATE EVANGELIUM*, ON THE ROMAN CURIA AND ITS SERVICE TO THE CHURCH AND TO THE WORLD, MARCH 19, 2022

The reform of the Roman Curia was among the issues the Cardinals outlined in the pre-conclave meetings in March 2013. Pope Francis worked on this all the nine years to its publication.

CD, 9 had called for reorganizing the Roman Curia to reflect the implications of episcopal collegiality decided by Vatican II. Paul VI answered with a reform of the Curia in his Apostolic Constitution *Regimini Ecclesiae Universae* (1967), changing the name, Supreme Congregation of the Holy Office, to Congregation for the Doctrine of the Faith. In 1988, John Paul II

---

10. John Paul II, *Ecclesia Dei*; Benedict XVI, *Summorum Pontificum*, and *Ecclesiae unitatem*.

promulgated his own Apostolic Constitution *Pastor Bonus*. Pope Francis's *Praedicate evangelium* (*Preach the Gospel*; henceforth *PE*) overrides both.

Undersecretaries, Synod of Bishops, Bp. Luis Marín de San Martín and Sr. Nathalie Becquart

Pope Francis already enacted some elements of the reform before the actual publication, which took effect on June 5, 2022.[11]

In 2015, and this for the first time, he named women theologians (five of them) among the thirty theologians of the International Theological Commission.

On June 23, 2018, he renamed the Secretariat for Communication, calling it the Dicastery for Communication. On July 5, 2018 (four years before the publication of *Praedicate Evangelium*), he appointed the lay journalist Paolo Ruffini as prefect of that dicastery, the first layman to head a Roman dicastery.

Sr. Raffaella Petrini became the first female secretary general of the administration of the Vatican City State. In February, 2021, Sr. Nathalie Becquart became the first female Undersecretary at the Synod of Bishops,

---

11. The author takes up some ideas already expressed in Okoye, "For a Synodal Church."

with the right of vote as *ex officio* member of the synod. Also Sr. Allessandra Smerrilli became the first female interim secretary of the Dicastery for Promoting Integral Human Development, a number two position in that Dicastery.[12]

On March 15, 2024, the appointment was announced of Colombian bishop Luis Manuel Ali Herrera as the new Secretary of the Pontifical Commission for the Protection of Minors. A new post of adjunct secretary was created and filled by a lay American woman, Teresa Morris Kettlekamp.[13] Both were already members of the Commission.

Pope Francis also anticipated the norms of *PE* by no longer making several heads of the Congregations Cardinals. He reformed the Curia along synodal lines, embedding themes outlined in *Evangelii gaudium*.

"The Roman Curia is composed of the Secretariat of State, the Dicasteries and other Institutions, all juridically equal among themselves" (Art. 12.1). Quite a few offices were merged, bringing the total of dicasteries to sixteen.[14] The terms *congregation* and *pontifical council* disappear. "Congregations"[15] exercised jurisdiction on behalf of the pope; "Councils" promoted various pastoral initiatives.[16] Each office of the Roman Curia is now called a dicastery, a term that suggests that in principle they are all equal, also that any of the baptized may be appointed to it.

> The Roman Curia is at the service of the Pope, who, as the successor of Peter, is the perpetual and visible source and foundation of the unity both of the bishops and of the whole company of the faithful. By virtue of this bond, the work of the Roman Curia is also organically related to the College of Bishops and individual bishops, as well as to episcopal conferences and their regional and continental groupings, and the hierarchical structures of the Eastern Churches . . . . The Roman Curia is not set between the pope and the bishops, but is at the service of both, according to the modalities proper to the nature of each (Preamble, no. 8).

---

12. *Tablet*, "First Female Secretary General," 26.

13. She was former executive director of the USCCB Secretariat of Child and Youth Protection. O'Connell, "Pope Francis Appoints."

14. Besides the Secretariat of State there were nine Congregations, twelve Pontifical Councils, three Tribunals, and a few other offices.

15. The term *congregation* derived from commissioning select groups of cardinals, drawn from the College of Cardinals, to take care of some field of activity that concerned the Holy See. The term implied that only cardinals could be head of that office.

16. de Souza, "10 Highlights of '*Praedicate evangelium*.'"

The present reform proposes, in the spirit of a "sound decentralization," to leave to the competence of bishops the authority to resolve, in the exercise of "their proper task as teachers" and pastors, those issues with which they are familiar and that do not affect the church's unity of doctrine, discipline, and communion, always acting with that spirit of co-responsibility which is the fruit and expression of the specific *mysterium communionis* that is the church (II, no. 2).

One recalls that the Preparatory Schema of Vatican II, *de Episcopis ac de diocesium regimine* (*Concerning Bishops and the Government of Dioceses*), April 1963, had clothed the Curia with the authority of the pope. In the Vatican II aula, on November 8, 1963, Cardinal Josef Frings received frenzied applause when he criticized this self-perception of the Roman Curia as being the voice box of the pope and the supreme authority in the church and its presumption to be judge over the opinions of the Vatican Council in session. The Curia, he said, should be internationalized, members of the Curia should not be consecrated bishops as reward for service, nor need Curia officers necessarily be priests; laypeople should also be appointed.[17] The cardinal already anticipated some of the ideas of *Praedicate evangelium* and the synod on synodality!

The head of every dicastery is uniformly called a Prefect. The Dicastery for Evangelization[18] takes pride of place (the "missionary option") and has the pope himself as prefect. He is assisted by two pro-prefects. Francis thus put evangelization at the heart of the Roman Curia, making himself "the chief missionary of a missionary church."[19] The Congregation for the Doctrine of the Faith, now Dicastery for the Doctrine of the Faith (DDF), had been known as "*La Suprema*" until 1968, with the pope himself as its head.

Pope Francis upgraded the Office of the Papal Almoner to the status of a Dicastery for the Service of Charity. It comes third (after the Dicastery for Evangelization and the Dicastery for the Doctrine of the Faith). The pope chose Konrad Krajewski to head this dicastery and created him a Cardinal, highlighting the service of charity (*diakonia*) as of the essential nature of the church and close to Francis' heart. During a vacancy (*sede vacante*), all prefects lose their office, except the Cardinal in charge of the Apostolic

---

17. See Rush, *Vision of Vatican II*, 328.

18. This combines the Pontifical Council for Promoting the New Evangelization (created by Benedict XVI in 2010) with the Congregation for Evangelization of Peoples.

19. de Souza, "10 Highlights of '*Praedicate Evangelium*.'"

Penitentiary (the "internal forum"). To this exception, Pope Francis now adds the papal almoner! The mercy of God and the service of charity are never to be interrupted.[20]

He also established a third section (new) of the Secretariat of State to care for the diplomatic personnel of the Holy See, thereby showing his pastoral concern.

> Each curial institution carries out its proper mission by virtue of the power it has received from the Roman Pontiff, in whose name it operates with vicarious power in the exercise of his primatial *munus*. For this reason, any member of the faithful can preside over a Dicastery or Office, depending on the power of governance and the specific competence and function of the dicastery or office in question. (II, no. 5)[21]

> The officials are selected, as far as possible, from various regions of the world, so that the Curia may reflect the universal character of the church. They are taken from among clerics, members of Institutes of Consecrated Life and Societies of Apostolic Life, and laity distinguished for their experience and proven expertise. (Art. 14.3)

> In choosing clerics as officials, care should be taken, as far as possible, to maintain a balance between diocesan or eparchial clerics and those of Institutes of Consecrated Life and Societies of Apostolic Life. (Art. 14.5)

> The consultors of curial institutions and offices are appointed from among the faithful who are distinguished by their expertise, proven ability, and prudence. (Art. 16)

> As a rule, after five years, clerical officials and members of Institutes of Consecrated Life and Societies of Apostolic Life who have served in curial institutions and offices are to return to their Diocese or Eparchy, or to the Institute or Society to which they belong to continue their pastoral work. If the Superiors of the Roman Curia deem it appropriate, their service can be extended for another five-year period. (Art. 17.4)

> Members who have reached eighty years of age cease from their appointment. (Art 17.3)

20. de Souza, "10 Highlights of '*Praedicate evangelium*.'"
21. Because members operate by vicarious power from the pope, any baptized can function in or head a dicastery. It is possible that the phrase "depending on the power of governance and the specific competence and function of the dicastery or office in question" aims at restricting to clerics the presidency over some offices, like DDF and Dicastery for Clergy.

Outstanding qualities are demanded for service in the Curia.

> Those who serve in the Curia are chosen from bishops, priests, deacons, members of Institutes of Consecrated Life and Societies of Apostolic Life, and lay men and women outstanding for their spiritual life, solid pastoral experience, simplicity of life and love for the poor, spirit of communion and service, competence in the matters entrusted to them, and ability to discern the signs of the times. (II, no. 7)

Episcopal conferences, mentioned sixty-six times, receive greater attention as a structure of synodality.

In conformity with the modification of canon 838.3 envisaged in his Motu Proprio *Magnum principium* of September 3, 2017, the Dicastery for Divine Worship and the Discipline of the Sacraments

> confirms the translations of liturgical books in current languages and grants the *recognitio* to the fitting adaptations of these to local cultures, as legitimately approved by the episcopal conferences. It also grants the *recognitio* to particular calendars and to the Proper of Masses and the Liturgy of the Hours of particular churches and Institutes of Consecrated Life and Societies of Apostolic Life, following their approval by the relative competent authority. (Art. 89.2)

The doctrine of *PE* was taken for granted in the *Instrumentum laboris* of the Synod on Synodality which mentioned it several times. As already mentioned, *PE* had already set out in practice some of the structures and processes still being debated, for example, concerning the empowerment of the lay faithful. The five-year rotation of people from all over the world will definitely enhance mutual relations between the local churches and Rome, bringing "*Romanitas*" back to the local churches.

## DEBATE ABOUT THE ORIGIN OF THE POWER OF GOVERNANCE IN THE CHURCH

It would seem that "each curial institution carries out its proper mission by virtue of the power it has received from the Roman Pontiff, in whose name it operates with vicarious power in the exercise of his primatial *munus*."[22] For *the Pillar*, that would be "a theological sea change" as it separates

---

22. *Pillar*, "What Is the 'Lay Governance' Debate?," §19.

sacramental ordination from the capability to hold church offices that exercise significant governance.

Cardinal Marcello Semeraro, Msgr. Marco Mellino, and Fr. Gianfranco Ghirlanda, SJ, presented this document to the media on March 21, 2022. Fr. Ghirlanda[23] explained that "the power of governance in the church does not come from the sacrament of Holy Orders, but from the canonical mission."[24] In a later article,[25] he interpreted *PE*, Preamble 5, to say that "every curial institution fulfils its mission by virtue of the power received from the Roman Pontiff in whose name it acts with vicarious power in the exercise of its *munus primaziale*." Lay people could fill those offices because the power associated with them is in fact papal power.[26] Further, "The vicarious power to carry out an office is the same if it is received by a bishop, a presbyter, a consecrated man or woman, or a lay man or woman."[27]

In a 1989 article, Fr. Ghirlanda had argued that the power of church governance had a non-sacramental origin. A pope who is not a bishop is able to be supreme pontiff immediately after election; he receives the supreme power through mission. Consecration is required by positive church law as a condition for the power of primacy to be exercised.[28] Because the power of governance in the church has non-sacramental origin, lay persons can be appointed by the competent hierarchical authority to offices not considered strictly clerical or hierarchical.[29] Hierarchical communion being organic, "a relationship of hierarchical subordination is set up between the Roman Pontiff and the bishops [such that] bishops receive this power [collegial power] through the Roman Pontiff who transmits—not delegates—such power to them." Canonical mission by the bishop confers

---

23. Pope Francis made the seventy-nine-year-old Cardinal in the Consistory of August 27, 2022, and appointed him to replace Cardinal Burke both in the Papal Signatura and as Patron of the Knights of Malta.

24. FSSPX News, "Reform of the Curia," §14. FSSPX is an organ of the Pius X schismatic group.

25. Ghirlanda, "Apostolic Constitution '*Praedicate Evangelium*.'"

26. Hahn, "*Potestas incerta*," 189. I cite the text from this source as Ghirlanda's article was not available to me online.

27. See Hahn, "*Potestas incerta*," 189.

28. Ghirlanda, "Universal Church, Particular Church," 265n115.

29. Ghirlanda, "Universal Church, Particular Church," 268. He cites the power of governance exercised in Institutes of Consecrated Life, including lay ones (canons 596; 618). The mitered abbess of past centuries sometimes exercised a kind of ordinary authority over church life in territory surrounding their monasteries.

an office (*munus*) and transmits the corresponding power of governance (he cites *LG*, 28).[30]

Such separation of governance from sacramental orders became a hot issue. Cardinal Kasper stressed that Vatican II "tends to reconnect the two areas and unite the two powers" of sacramental and governing authority. For him,

> A dualism between the authority sacramentally conferred by ordination and the authority of governance or jurisdiction conferred by mandate could end up becoming detached from the sacramental life of the church and could also develop a certain life of its own with unhappy consequences.[31]

Cardinal Ouellet, Prefect of the Dicastery for Bishops, opined that:

> As for the government of the Roman curia, it is not enough to say that the canonical mission entrusted by the Holy Father is sufficient to establish the power of jurisdiction of every authority exercised in the dicasteries, be it the person designated cardinal, bishop, religious or lay person. [To do so would perpetuate] a juridical mentality . . . which places the emphasis only on the delegation of power, without taking into account the charismatic dimension of the church, which would go directly against the opening to authentic decentralization.[32]

Canon Law itself, which enacted the documents of Vatican II into law, is not consistent on the matter. Canon 129 states:

> Those who are in sacred orders are, in accordance with the provisions of law, capable (*habiles sunt*) of the power of governance which belongs to the church by divine institution. This power is also called the power of jurisdiction (§1).[33]
>
> Lay members of Christ's faithful can cooperate (*cooperari*) in the exercise of this same power in accordance with the law (§2).

Canon 274.1 legislates:

> Only clerics can obtain offices the exercise of which requires the power of order or the power of ecclesiastical governance.

---

30. Ghirlanda, "Universal Church, Particular Church," 252.
31. Pillar, "What Is the 'Lay Governance' Debate?," §41.
32. Pillar, "What Is the 'Lay Governance' Debate?," §38–39.
33. This reflects canon 118 of the 1917 Code: "Clerics alone are capable of obtaining the power or order or of ecclesiastical jurisdiction."

Both norms seem to be in conflict: "The apparently conflicting canons [129.1 and 274.1] represent a compromise in relation to the as yet unresolved theological dispute about the nature and origin of sacred power in the church and the accessibility of that power to the laity."[34]

This may be a case of the legislator's studied ambiguity. The draft of canon 129.2 had *partem habere* ("participate"), which was changed to *cooperari* in the final promulgated text. It is "co-competence," but the basis and extent remain unclear.[35] At the 1981 Plenary Congregation of the Commission on the Reform of the Code, Cardinal Ratzinger dubbed the idea that lay people could exercise a power they do not possess a "logical contradiction."[36] Yet, in canon 545.1,[37] "cooperating" seems synonymous with "participating." Two approaches have been made in interpreting the *cooperari* of canon 129.2.

> The Council neither intended nor spoke about the power of jurisdiction of laity. However, historically laity exercised such power.[38] The Council had no intention to break with history. Hence laity can exercise the power of jurisdiction. [This is dubbed the Roman School].

> The Council decided on the oneness of power, the only source being ordination. Laity cannot exercise the power of jurisdiction. *Cooperari* must be interpreted in terms of preparation, accompaniment, and execution of acts of jurisdiction.[39] [This is dubbed the Munich School].

---

34. Beal et al., *New Commentary*, 348.

35. Hahn, "*Potestas incerta*," 187.

36. See Hahn, "*Potestas incerta*," 185.

37. "Whenever it is necessary or opportune for the due pastoral care of the parish, one or more assistant priests can be joined with the parish priest. As cooperators with the parish priest and sharers in his concern (*tanquam parochi cooperators eiusque sollicitudinis participes*)."

38. The list is long: office of ecclesiastical judge (canon 1421; though see Ratzinger's comment above); promoters of justice (canon 1435); defenders of the bond (canon 1435); laity may prepare couples for marriage and formally assist at weddings (canon 112.1); with consent of the pastor, laity may preach after the Gospel (Masses with Children, no. 24); diocesan finance officer (canon 494); finance officer of a religious institution (canon 636); lay persons leading parishes (canon 517.2); lay administrators of church goods (canon 1279). See Beal et al., *New Commentary*, 349–350; Hahn, "*Potestas incerta*," 188.

39. Beal et al., *New Commentary*, 185.

# 4

# The Documents of the 2023 Synod

## THE *PREPARATORY DOCUMENT*[1] AND THE *HANDBOOK*[2]

THE *HANDBOOK* LAYS OUT the objectives of the synodal process and the method of its preparation. The purpose is not to produce documents but,

> to plant dreams, draw forth prophecies and visions, allow hope to flourish, inspire trust, bind up wounds, weave together relationships, awaken a dawn of hope, learn from one another and create a bright resourcefulness that will enlighten minds, warm hearts, give strength to our hands.[3]

Nor is the synodal process an opportunity to provide a temporary or one-time experience of synodality, but rather to provide an opportunity for the entire People of God to discern together how to move forward on the path towards being a more synodal church in the long term (*Handbook* 9.1.3).

The entire People of God discerns together. The synodal process is thus a journey for all the faithful, no longer an assembly of only bishops. Every local church has an integral part to play. The teaching authority of the pope and the bishops is in dialogue with the *sensus fidelium* [sense of

---

1. Synod of Bishops, *Preparatory Document for the 16th Ordinary General Assembly*.
2. Synod of Bishops, *Vademecum for the Synod on Synodality*.
3. Francis, "Address at the Opening of the Synod on Young People"; also *PD*, 32.

the faith], the living voice of the People of God.[4] Collaborating with theologians—lay, ordained, and religious—can be a helpful support in articulating the voice of the People of God expressing the reality of the faith on the basis of lived experience (*Handbook* 1.3). Communities of consecrated men and women, the various movements and the new ecclesial communities, all used to synodal processes, can offer their experience of discernment and synodal approaches.[5] Two fundamental questions are proposed for our discernment:

> How does this "journeying together" take place today on different levels (from the local level to the universal one), allowing the church to proclaim the Gospel? And what steps is the Spirit inviting us to take in order to grow as a synodal church? (*PD*, 2; *Handbook* 1.3)

In responding to these questions, people are invited to do the following.

> Ask yourself what experiences in your particular church the fundamental question calls to mind;
>
> Re-read these experiences in greater depth: What joys did they provoke? What difficulties and obstacles have they encountered? What wounds have they brought to light? What insights have they elicited?
>
> Gather the fruits to share. Where in these experiences does the voice of the Spirit resound? What is he asking of us? What are the points to be confirmed, the prospects for change, the steps to be taken? Where do we register a consensus? What paths are opening up for our particular church? (*PD*, 26; *Handbook* 5.3)
>
> The synodal process is first and foremost a *spiritual* process . . . [and] not a mechanical data-gathering exercise or a series of meetings and debates; it is oriented towards *discernment*. . . . If listening is the method of the synodal process, and discerning the aim, participation is the path. Fostering participation leads us out of ourselves to involve others who hold different views than we do. (*Handbook* 2.2; italics added)
>
> Special care should be taken to involve those persons who may risk being excluded: women, the handicapped, refugees, migrants, the elderly, people who live in poverty, Catholics who rarely or

---

4. ITC, *Sensus Fidei in the Life of the Church*, 74.
5. ITC, *Synodality*, 74; also *Handbook*, 1.5.

> never practice their faith ... Creative means should also be found in order to involve children and youth. (*Handbook*, 2.1)
>
> A synodal process is a time to dialogue with people from the worlds of economics and science, politics and culture, arts and sport, the media and social initiatives. It will be a time to reflect on ecology and peace, life issues and migration ... It is also an opportunity to deepen the ecumenical journey with other Christian denominations and to deepen our understanding with other faith traditions (*Handbook*, 2.4).

Temptations and pitfalls to be avoided include: seeing only the problems and fixating on them (we can miss the light if we focus only on the darkness); focusing only on structures; the temptation of conflict and division, or treating the synod as a kind of parliament in which one side must defeat the other; wanting to lead ourselves instead of being led by God (*Handbook* 2.4).

## PREPARATION IN PRACTICE

A synthesis of not more than ten pages is to be prepared by each diocese and ultimately for each episcopal conference.

> The synthesis does not only report common trends and points of convergence, but also highlights those points that strike a chord, inspire an original point of view, or open a new horizon. The synthesis should pay special attention to the voices of those who are not often heard and integrate what could be called the "minority report." The feedback should not only underline positive experiences but also bring to light challenging and negative experiences in order to reflect the reality of what has been listened to. (*Handbook*, 4.1)

The "key role of the bishop is *to listen*." Of course, he may review the feedback from the consultations, "discerning what the Holy Spirit is saying through the people entrusted to his care" (*Handbook* 4.2). He is to appoint a diocesan contact person/team, who may be priests, religious, or lay persons (who are given training and personal support in form of budgets, physical facilities, online platforms) and suggest to parishes and communities to appoint their own contact persons/teams to collaborate in the consultation. It is recommended that the co-leaders be one man and one woman; at least one of them should be a lay person.

The contact persons should be adorned with many spiritual qualities. They are to be, people of prayer who promote a genuinely spiritual experience of synodality; persons with a living faith; natural collaborators; effective communicators; able to synthesize a variety of information; able to interact well with people of diverse cultural, generational, and ecclesial backgrounds; familiar with diocesan structures and processes; humble in working with a co-leader and/or team; and graciously open to the insights and gifts of others as well as trying new ways of proceeding (*Handbook*, appendix A).

## THE WORKING DOCUMENT FOR THE CONTINENTAL STAGE

### Lights

The Working Document synthesizes the reports from the national episcopal conferences. Participation exceeded expectation. The "Synod Secretariat received summaries from 112 out 114 episcopal conferences and from all the 15 Oriental Catholic Churches." From the Roman Curia, seventeen out of twenty-three dicasteries sent in reflections, as did the USG/UISG (Religious Superiors of Men and Religious Superiors of Women) "and lay movements and associations of the faithful. Over one thousand contributions arrived from individuals and groups," besides insights gathered through the Digital Synod (no. 5).

Frankness and love of the church characterized the reports. With *parrhesia*, the reports named the "lights and shadows" of the church (no. 17). For many, this was the first time the church had asked for their opinion; they appreciated "the uniqueness of speaking freely and being heard in organized conversations that were open-ended" (no. 23; Ep. Conf.[6] Pakistan). "Some Christians who felt hurt and had distanced themselves from the church came back during this consultative phase" (no. 17; Ep. Conf. Central African Republic). Several reports highlighted "the strengthened feeling of belonging to the church and the realisation on a practical level that the church is not just priests and bishops" (no. 16; Ep. Conf. Bangladesh). The synod experience awakened a desire to "get involved in the life of the church, in its engagement with the world today, and in its pastoral work on the ground" (no. 15; Ep. Conf. Canada). There is a strong mobilization

---

6. Ep. Conf. stands for Episcopal Conference.

of the People of God, the joy of coming together, of walking together and of speaking freely. "This kind of cooperation should become the 'unwritten laws' of church culture" (no. 17; Ep. Conf. Latvia).

The image of "tent" in Isa 54:2 evoked the tent of meeting that accompanied the People of God on the journey through the desert. At the center the Lord was present. The tent needs to be spread out to also protect those still outside its space, but who feel called to enter it (no. 26). "The world needs a 'church that goes forth,' that rejects the division between believers and non-believers, that looks at humanity and offers it more than a doctrine or a strategy, an experience of salvation . . . that responds to the cry of humanity and nature" (no. 42; Ep. Conf. Portugal). "Instead of behaving like gate-keepers trying to exclude others from the table" (no. 31; Ep. Conf. USA), "the church is called to more fully live the Christological paradox: boldly proclaiming its authentic teaching while at the same time offering a witness of radical inclusion and acceptance through its pastoral and discerning accompaniment" (no. 30; Ep. Conf. England and Wales).

## Shadows

There was difficulty understanding what synodality meant, failure in some places to organize synodal gatherings, and even outright resistance to the basic proposal. For example, an individual submission from the UK wrote, "I distrust the synod. I think it has been called to bring about further change to Christ's teachings and wound his church further" (no. 18). Some feared that the procedures imitated a democratic-type majority principle. Others despaired of any outcome, seeing "the church as a rigid institution unwilling to change," or perhaps the outcome was already predetermined (no. 18; Ep. Conf. Canada). Mentioned was the difficulty of listening deeply and accepting being transformed by it and the need for training in this area. "The laity feel that the flight from sincere listening stems from fear of having to engage pastorally" (no. 33; Ep. Conf. Poland). Resistance on the part of the clergy was reported' "also the passivity of the laity and their fear of expressing themselves freely" (no. 19). Several reports complain about the lack or weak involvement of priests (no. 19; Ep. Conf. Chile).

Many local churches sadly noted the voices absent from the synod process: the poor on the peripheries and in most remote places, "the lonely elderly, indigenous peoples, migrants without any affiliation and who lead a precarious existence, street children, alcoholics and drug addicts, those trapped in criminality, those for whom prostitution seems their only chance of survival, victims of trafficking" (no. 40).

## Challenges

The path to greater inclusion "begins with listening and requires a broader and deeper conversion of attitudes and structures, also new approaches to pastoral accompaniment." We need to "recognize others as subjects of their own journey," so they "feel welcomed, not judged." Some laity, deacons, and religious men and women have "the feeling that the institutional church was not interested in their faith experience or their opinions" (no. 32).

The scandal of clergy abuse is "an open wound that continues to inflict pain on victims," survivors, and their families. For many, this is still a powerful and unresolved issue (no. 20). "Many local churches express concern about the impact of a lack of trust and credibility" deriving from it (no. 51). "Some dioceses reported that participants wished for them publicly to acknowledge and atone for past abuses" (no. 20; Ep. Conf. Australia).

"In some of our countries the major threat is the ocean as changes in climate have drastic outcomes for the actual survival of these countries" (no. 45; Ep. Conf. Pacific).

The synod and its theme of communion call for authentic healing of the collective memory, also that the "pastoral of unity and reconciliation" between the Tutsi and the Hutu "must continue to be a priority" (no. 21; Ep. Conf. Rwanda). The church has an important role in the public sphere particularly in peace-building and reconciliation. In heavily divided societies this is often seen as a crucial part of mission (no. 46; Catholic Armenian Church).

Many noted "the challenges of tribalism, sectarianism, racism, poverty and gender inequality within the life of the church, as well as the world." "The rich and the educated are listened to more than others" (no. 44; Uganda). In some places, "historical entanglements between the church and political power continue to have an effect on the mission context" (no. 51; Malta).

"There are countries where Christians, especially young people, face the challenge of systematic forced conversion to other religions. . . . In such cases, walking together with people of other faiths, instead of retreating behind the wall of separation, requires the courage of prophecy" (no. 52).

There is no complete synodality without unity among Christians. In some places there is an "ecumenism of martyrdom" where persecution continues to unite Christians. The church is called to give "greater attention to divisive realities, for example the question of sharing the Eucharist" (no. 48; Ep. Conf. Republic of Central Africa). Many local churches with numerous Christian denominations place particular stress on "the baptismal dignity of all Christian brothers and sisters, and the common mission in the service of the gospel." They express a desire for "deeper ecumenical encounter and the need for formation to support this work" (no. 22; Ep. Conf. Japan).

A synodal church calls for a more meaningful intercultural approach. "The encounter between the Catholic Church in Cambodia and the Buddhist Monks and lay Cambodian Buddhists creates a new culture. All our activities affect each other and affect the whole world. We may differ in religion, but we all seek the common good" (no. 53; Ep. Conf. Laos and Cambodia). The "porosity" of our churches means that lines "of demarcation with civil society is less marked than elsewhere. . . . We are always 'in the home of others' and this has taught us listening, flexibility, and creativity in forms, language, and practices" (no. 53; Ep. Conf. North African Region).

Universal concern was shown "regarding the meagre presence of the voice of young people in the synod process, as well as increasingly in the life of the church." An urgent need is a "renewed focus on young people, their formation and accompaniment." "Since our young people experience a high degree of alienation, we need to make a preferential option for the young" (no. 35; Antilles).

> Many reports express . . . concern for the pressures experienced by families and the resulting impact on intergenerational relationships and faith transmission. Many Asian reports ask for better accompaniment and formation for families, as they negotiate changing cultural conditions (no. 51).

The "shortage of priests and the increasing loss of volunteers lead to priests' exhaustion"; besides, "they do not always feel heard; some see their ministry questioned." There is need to discuss why fewer and fewer feel called to the priesthood (no. 19; Ep. Conf. Austria). The reports note the "loneliness and isolation of many members of the clergy, who do not feel listened to, supported and appreciated." The voice of priests and bishops "speaking for themselves and their experience of walking together" seems lacking (no. 34). While many expressed deep appreciation and affection for the faithful and dedicated priests, they also voiced a desire for better formed, better accompanied, and less isolated priests.

There is need for "appropriate forms of welcome and protection for the women and eventual children of priests" who are at the risk of suffering serious injustice and discrimination (no. 34). Those who have left ordained ministry and married "ask for a more welcoming church, with greater willingness to dialogue" (no. 39).

People who "feel a tension between belonging to the church and their own loving relationships seek meaningful dialogue and a more welcome space: remarried divorcees, single parents, people living in polygamous marriage, LGBTQ people, etc." Attitudes vary. On the one hand, "People ask that the church be a refuge for the wounded and broken, not an institution for the perfect. They want the church . . . to walk with them rather than judge them" (no. 39; Ep. Conf. USA). On the other hand, "There is a new phenomenon in the church that is absolutely new in Lesotho: same-sex relationships . . . Surprisingly, there are Catholics in Lesotho who have started practicing this behavior and expect the church to accept them and their way of behaving" (no. 39; Ep. Conf. Lesotho). South Africa notes differing views, and hence the inability to give a definitive community stance, on such issues as the church's teaching on abortion, divorce and remarriage, Holy Communion, homosexuality, and LGBTQIA+ (no. 51; Ep. Conf. South Africa).

A special phenomenon is that of female migration and "women who decide to have an abortion due to fear of material poverty and rejection by their families" (no. 37; Ukrainian Greek Catholic Church).

"The universal church must remain the guarantor of unity, but dioceses can inculturate the faith locally: decentralization is necessary" (no. 54; Archdiocese of Luxembourg).

The church needs be rid of clericalism, so all Christ's faithful can together fulfill the common mission. "Some parish priests behave like 'order-givers,' imposing their will without listening to anyone." Clericalism can be as much a temptation for lay people as for clergy (no. 58; Central African Republic). The mission of the church is realized through the lives of all the baptized. The reports affirm the value of all vocations in the church and invite us to follow Jesus' manner of exercising power and authority in the church. "It is important to build a synodal institutional model as an ecclesial paradigm of deconstructing pyramidal power that privileges unipersonal managements" (no. 57; Ep. Conf. Argentina).

The reports "express a deep and energetic desire for renewed forms of leadership—priestly, episcopal, religious, and lay—that are relational and collaborative, and forms of authority capable of generating solidarity and co-responsibility" (no. 59; Ep. Conf. Slovakia).

The experience "has helped to rediscover the co-responsibility that comes from baptismal dignity and has let emerge the possibility of overcoming a vision of church built around ordained ministry in order to move toward a church that is 'all ministerial,' which is a communion of different charisms and ministries" (no. 67; Ep. Conf. Italy). But, the question needs be answered, "What concrete tasks can the laity perform? How is the responsibility of the baptized articulated with that of the parish priest?" (no. 68; Ep. Conf. Belgium).

"While maintaining their collegiality and freedom of decision-making that is devoid of any kind of pressure, the episcopal conferences should include representatives of the clergy and laity of the various dioceses in their debates and meetings" (no. 75; Secretariat of State, Section for the Diplomatic Staff of the Holy See). Diocesan and parish pastoral and economic councils, along with the episcopal and presbyteral councils, should be not only consultative, "but places where decisions are made on the basis of processes of communal discernment rather than on the majority principle used in democratic regimes" (no. 78).

Numbers 60 to 65 rethink women's participation in the church. Women are baptized and equal members of the People of God. They represent the "majority of practising members and are among the most active members of the church" (no. 61; Ep. Conf. Korea). Unfortunately, "sexism in decision-making and church language is prevalent in the church . . . women are excluded from meaningful roles . . . discriminated against by not receiving a fair wage for their ministries and services" (no. 63; Superiors of Institutes of Consecrated Life). "The reports do not agree on a single response to the question of the vocation, inclusion and flourishing of women in church" and society, including the active role of women in the governing structures of church bodies, the possibility for women with adequate training to preach in parish settings, and a female diaconate. "Much greater diversity of opinion was expressed on the subject of priestly ordination for women, which some reports call for, while others consider a closed issue" (no. 64).

For the process of synodality to continue, "a change of mindset and a renewal of existing structures are needed" (no. 72; Ep. Conf. India). "This new vision will need to be supported by a spirituality that will sustain the practice of synodality" (no. 72). "The overwhelming majority of reports indicate the need to provide for formation in synodality. Structures alone are not enough" (no. 82). A synodal spirituality welcomes differences and promotes harmony; it is a spirituality of "we" which can enhance the contributions of each person (no. 82). Formation in synodality is critical for those who will be called to assume leadership roles, especially priests (no. 83; Ep. Conf. Sri Lanka). "Spiritual discernment must accompany strategic planning and decision-making, so that each project is welcomed and accompanied by the Holy Spirit" (no. 84; Greek Melkite Catholic Church).

All church institutions, especially universities and academic institutions, are called to renew their structures and procedures according to the spirit of synodality. "In particular, theological faculties will be able to deepen the ecclesiological Christological and Pneumatological insights that synodal experiences and practices bring" (no. 80).

"Many people [ask] to promote and evangelize [popular religiosity] with a view to a more intense participation and a conscious incorporation into Christian life" (no. 90; Ep. Conf. Panama). There is need to rethink a liturgy too concentrated on the celebrant and to promote a liturgy "more alive and participatory of all the community of believers, priests, laity, youth, and children" (no. 91; Ep. Conf. Ethiopia). The quality of homilies is almost unanimously reported as a problem; there is call for "deeper homilies, centered on the Gospel and the readings of the day, and not on politics" (no. 93; Maronite Church). Several reports noted the "incomprehensibility of the language normally used by the church" (no. 95; Ep. Conf. France).

"The limited access to the 1962 Missal was lamented; many felt that the differences over how to celebrate the liturgy sometimes reached the level of animosity" (no. 92; Ep. Conf. USA).

Access to the Eucharist is limited for communities in very remote areas, "also by the use of charging fees for access to celebrations, which discriminate against the poorest" (no. 94). As to access for divorced and remarried, "some expressed the view that the church should be more flexible," others that the practice of exclusion should continue (no. 94; Ep. Conf. Malaysia).

## THREE QUESTIONS TO FOCUS ON

> After having read and prayed with the DCS, which intuitions resonate most strongly with the lived experiences and realities of

> the church in your continent? Which experiences are new, or illuminating to you?
>
> After having read and prayed with the DCS, what substantial tensions or divergences emerge as particularly important in your continent's perspective? Consequently, what are the questions or issues that should be addressed and considered in the next steps of the process?
>
> Looking at what emerges from the previous two questions, what are the priorities, recurring themes and calls to action that can be shared with other local churches around the world and discussed during the First Session of the Synodal Assembly in October 2023? (no. 106)

The seven Continental Assemblies were asked to send back their reports to the Synod Secretariat by March 31, 2023. The seven are: Middle East, Europe, Asia, North America, Latin America and Caribbean, Africa and Madagascar, and Oceania. There was also the document for the Digital Synod.

## TWO SESSIONS OF THE SYNOD ON SYNODALITY ANNOUNCED

In his Angelus Address on October 16, 2022, Pope Francis split the Universal Stage of the Synod into two sessions, both meeting in Rome—October 2023 and October 2024.

Pope Francis had tried out the idea of two sessions during the Synod on the Family held in two consecutive years, 2014 and 2015, all within the current structure of the Synod of Bishops. The sharp exchanges of the first session mellowed somewhat into broader consensus in the second. Though disagreements remained on several topics (the internal forum for divorced and remarried, same-sex couples and their pastoral care, conscience and positive law . . .), the bishops found common ground enough to reach the required two-thirds majority on many topics. Pope Francis wrote: "We have been called to form consciences, not to replace them" (*AL*, no. 37). He spoke of the need to be humble and acknowledge that at times the way we present our Christian beliefs and treat other people has helped contribute to today's problematic situation. "We often present marriage in such a way that its unitive meaning and ideal of mutual assistance are overshadowed by an almost exclusive insistence on the duty of procreation" (*AL*, no. 36).

In short, the church needs to *listen* to the concrete experiences of the faithful and discern accordingly.

## SECAM: RESPONSE TO DOCUMENT FOR THE CONTINENTAL STAGE

As example of the responses from the Continental Episcopal Conferences, I mention some SECAM highlights that respond to particular situations in Africa and Madagascar.

Teams of bishops, religious, and lay faithful met in Accra (December 2022) and Nairobi to reread the *DCS* document in the context of the Church in Africa. Finally, in Addis Ababa (March 2023) about two hundred "Cardinals, Archbishops, Bishops, Priests, Religious men and women, and Lay faithful" (the lay faithful being in greater number) met and issued the Final Document of SECAM (March 6, 2023) to be fed into the *Instrumentum laboris* of the synod.[7]

> The church came with a culture into another culture. Synodality should help to listen to the cultural practices that have been either ignored, condemned, or suppressed by the Western culture through which the Gospel was preached to Africans. They should, therefore, be listened to in view of either integrating, purifying, or collectively rejecting them based on a clear understanding of the exigencies of the Gospel.[8]
>
> The process of synodality must also involve inculturation and liturgical renewal . . . . The current ways of celebrating the liturgy sometimes leave many Africans unfulfilled. A synodal church should take into consideration the nature of Africans to have a more participatory liturgy, in line with authentic liturgical theology and doctrine.[9]

The image of the church as Family of God calls for inclusivity to be harmonized with conversion, "since walking together in communion, participation, and mission cannot be divorced from evangelisation . . . [and] the need to help people abandon their old ways that are not in conformity with the Word of God and embrace the truth of the Gospel."[10]

---

7. SECAM, "Document of the African Synodal Continental Assembly," 2.
8. SECAM, "Document of the African Synodal Continental Assembly," 6.
9. SECAM, "Document of the African Synodal Continental Assembly," 12.
10. SECAM, "Document of the African Synodal Continental Assembly," 7.

At the level of solidarity, we are weak: a problem in Uganda should be of concern to Algeria. A synodal African Church should be able to unite Africans.[11] [Hence] the need for the synodal church to work together with other faith communities in the promotion of peace and conflict resolution in building the kingdom of God on earth.[12]

"The need for church authorities to engage the political leadership of the society in advocacy for good governance and justice . . . should be seen as part of the missionary mandate of making Christ known to the world."[13]

"African voices and values should be taken into consideration when elaborating the doctrines and teachings of the church, values such as family, solidarity, communitarian life, reverential dialogue, hospitality and co-responsibility."[14]

---

11. SECAM, "Document of the African Synodal Continental Assembly," 9.
12. SECAM, "Document of the African Synodal Continental Assembly," 11.
13. SECAM, "Document of the African Synodal Continental Assembly," 10.
14. SECAM, "Document of the African Synodal Continental Assembly," 11.

# 5

# The Documents: *Instrumentum laboris*

THE *INSTRUMENTUM LABORIS* (HENCEFORTH *IL*) for the October 2023 Synod was compiled by the Synod Secretariat from the reports of the Continental Assemblies and issued by the Synod Secretariat on June 20, 2023. It has a theological introduction (dated May 28, 2023) and fifteen worksheets, five worksheets for each of the three themes of the synod. The 2023 October Assembly addressed the topics in the order in which the *IL* proposed them.

## THEOLOGICAL INTRODUCTION

This has two parts marked A, "For a Synodal Church" (nos. 17–42) and B, "Communion, Mission, Participation" (nos. 43–60). Section A outlines fundamental characteristics of a synodal church and its manner of proceeding (conversation in the Spirit covers nos. 32–42). Section B articulates what emerges from the work of the Continental Stage.

Number 44 explains why the ordering of the three priorities has changed so that mission now has the central place (see below).

The priorities that emerged from listening to the People of God are not presented as assertions or stances (no. 10). Divisive language is avoided in order to promote better dialogue among members from different regions or traditions (no. 12). Effort has been made to lay out the shared questions, insights, and tensions that emerged. The tensions invite ongoing synodal discernment so as to become sources of energy and not lapse into destructive polarizations (no. 6). That questions continue to be asked about what is already received magisterial teaching should not surprise us. This is the case, for example, in the acceptance of remarried divorcees (in *Amoris laetitia*) and the inculturation of the liturgy (in the Instruction *Varietates legitimae*, 1994 of the Congregation for Divine Worship and the Discipline of the Sacraments). "The synodal assembly is a privileged forum" for discerning the real or perceived obstacles to the acceptance of magisterial teaching.

Synodality has begun to be embodied in the concrete experience of "constructive, respectful, and prayerful speaking, listening and dialogue" (no. 18). In listening to one another the members are gradually transformed by the Spirit, and "necessary changes in rules, structures, and procedures" (no. 15) suggest themselves, leading to "a church that is also increasingly synodal in its institutions, structures and procedures" (no. 21).

Yet, "synodal life is not a strategy for organizing the church, but the experience of being able to find a unity that embraces diversity without erasing it, because it is founded on union with God in the confession of the same faith. This dynamism possesses an impelling force that continually seeks to widen the scope of communion, but which must come to terms with the contradictions, limits, and wounds of history" (no. 49).

A synodal church "is not afraid of the variety it bears, but values it without forcing it into uniformity" (no. 25). The synodal process has been an opportunity to learn what it means to live unity in diversity: "no one is asked to leave their own context, but rather to understand it and enter into it more deeply" (no. 25). "The transition to the 'we' [should] not absorb the 'I' into the anonymity of an indistinct collectivity. [Participation] guards against falling into the abstractness of rights or reducing persons to subservient instruments for the organization's performance" (no. 56).

"The radical nature of Christianity is not the prerogative of a few specific vocations" (no. 26): all are called to be "an outgoing church," to build community together. "Mission is not the marketing of a religious product, but the construction of a community in which relationships are a manifestation of God's love and whose very life becomes therefore a proclamation" (no. 52; cf. Acts 2:42–47). A missionary synodal church "is able to solicit the contribution of all, each with their gifts and roles, valuing the diversity of charisms and integrating the relationship between hierarchical and charismatic gifts" (no. 54).

The different ordering, with mission at the center (no. 44), invites us "to move beyond a dualist understanding in which the relationships within the ecclesial community are the domain of communion, while mission concerns the momentum *ad extra*." There is growing awareness that "the orientation for mission is the only evangelically founded criterion for the internal organization of the Christian community, the distribution of roles and tasks, and the management of its institutions and structures." "Communion and mission are profoundly connected with each other, they interpenetrate and mutually imply each other, to the point that communion represents both the source and the fruit of mission: communion gives rise to mission and mission is accomplished in communion"[1] (no. 44). Because baptism confers common dignity to all children of God, thus creating a true co-responsibility among all members of the church, "a synodal church cannot be understood other than within the horizon of communion, which is always also a mission to proclaim and incarnate the Gospel in every dimension of human existence" (no. 20).

Integral participation and co-responsibility in mission raise "the question of authority, its meaning and the style of its exercise within a synodal church. In particular, does authority arise as a form of power derived from the models offered by the world, or is it rooted in service?" (cf. Mark 10:43; John 13:15; no. 57). "In its origin, the term 'authority' indicates the capacity to enable others to grow" (no. 57).

"A synodal church confronts honestly and fearlessly the call to a deeper understanding of the relationship between love and truth" (no. 57): "But speaking the truth in love, we must grow up in every way into him who is the head, into Christ" (Eph 4:15–16). A mark of a synodal church is "the ability to manage tensions without being crushed by them" (no. 28). Authentic listening leads to ways to continue walking together beyond fragmentation and polarization.

A synodal church, freed from "the anxiety of inadequacy," embraces "the healthy restlessness of incompleteness" (no. 29). Accepting its own vulnerabilities and submitting to the action of the Holy Spirit, it can afford the time it takes for discernment of the signs of the times, without rushing to immediate solutions (nos. 31, 29).

The theme of formation appears across all the documents of the first phase; institutions and structures alone are not enough to make the church synodal. "A synodal culture and spirituality are needed, animated by a desire for conversion and sustained by adequate formation" (58). "We need integral formation, initial and ongoing, for all members of the People of God. . . . Formation for a more genuinely synodal spirituality is at the

---

1. John Paul II, *Christifideles laici*, no. 32; *PE* I, 4.

heart of the renewal of the church" (no. 59). "Formation for conversation in the Spirit is formation to be a synodal church" (no. 42). "Candidates for ordained ministry must be trained in a synodal style and mentality. The promotion of a culture of synodality implies the renewal of the current seminary curriculum and the formation of teachers and professors of theology" (no. 59).

"Bishops, priests, deacons, consecrated men and women, and all those who exercise a ministry need formation to renew the ways of exercising authority and decision-making processes in a synodal key, and to learn how to accompany community discernment and conversation in the Spirit" (no. 59).

"Numerous contributions highlight the need for a similar effort to renew the language used by the church in its liturgy, preaching, catechesis, sacred art, as well as in all forms of communication addressed to the faithful and the wider public" (no. 60).

"The protagonist of the synod is the Holy Spirit" (no. 17). Conversation in the Spirit (outlined in nos. 32–42) is the "synodal method," which will be used in the synod assembly itself (see diagram below).[2] Though "pioneered by people formed in Ignatian spirituality, Conversation in the Spirit does not go back all the way to St. Ignatius of Loyola, the founder of the Jesuit order who developed the discernment of spirits." It appears to have been "first developed several decades ago by Jesuits in Canada," so some call it the "Canadian model," explains Fr. Anthony Lusvardi, SJ, professor of sacramental theology at the Pontifical Gregorian University in Rome.[3]

The coming assembly will gather the fruits of the process, discerning the paths we will continue to walk together. The assembly will consider ways to continue reading the experience of the People of God, including through promoting the necessary in-depth theological and canonical studies in preparation for the second session of the synodal assembly in October 2024.

2. Taken from p. 16 of the *IL* by permission.

3. Brockhaus, "Synod on Synodality's Listening 'Method,'" §§5–6. Lusvardi pointed out that "while it is great for helping people understand one another better, 'it is not well-suited for careful or complex theological or practical reasoning.' Doing that requires thinking that is critical, that weighs the pros and cons of what people say. It also requires a degree of objectivity that this method is not well-suited to provide. . . . Sound theology needs to always ask the question, "That may sound good, but is it true?"'" (Brockhaus, "Synod on Synodality's Listening 'Method,'" §§20–21).

## THE DOCUMENTS: INSTRUMENTUM LABORIS

# The conversation in the Spirit

**A dynamic of discernment in the synodal Church**

### PERSONAL PREPARATION

By entrusting oneself to the Father, conversing in prayer with the Lord Jesus and listening to the Holy Spirit, each one prepares his or her own contribution to the question about which he or she is called to discern.

**Silence, prayer and listening to the Word of God**

### «Taking the word and listening»

Each person takes turns speaking from his or her own experience and prayer, and listens carefully to the contribution of others.

**Silence and Prayer**

### «Making space for others and the Other»

From what the others have said, each one shares what has resonated most with him or her or what has aroused the most resistance in him or her, allowing himself or herself to be guided by the Holy Spirit: "When, listening, did my heart burn within me?"

**Silence and Prayer**

### «Building together»

Together we dialogue on the basis of what emerged earlier in order to discern and gather the fruit of the conversation in the Spirit: to recognize intuitions and convergences; to identify discordances, obstacles and new questions; to allow prophetic voices to emerge. It is important that everyone can feel represented by the outcome of the work. "To what steps is the Holy Spirit calling us together?"

### Final prayer of thanksgiving

**Conversation in the Spirit**

## THE WORKSHEETS

Fifteen worksheets, five worksheets for each of the three priorities, analyze the questions further. Perspectives outlined in the theological Introduction become "points of entry" to address the basic question of how the "journeying together" allows the church to proclaim the gospel and what steps the Spirit invites us to take in order to grow as a synodal church (cf. *PD*, 2). The many overlaps between these worksheets highlight "the rich network of interconnections between the topics covered." Each of the fifteen follows this outline:

> Enunciation of the topic
>
> Question for discernment
>
> Suggestions for prayer and preparatory reflection[4]

For reasons of space and for focus, I highlight only some proposals; even then I often abbreviate or alter the text somewhat. I give the three priorities and the five worksheets for each, then the suggestions and questions under each priority.

### B 1: A Communion that Radiates: How can we be more fully a Sign and Instrument of Union with God and of the Unity of Humanity?

> B 1.1 How does the service of charity and commitment to justice and care for our common home nourish communion in a synodal Church?
>
> B 1.2 How can a synodal church make credible the promise that "love and truth will meet" (Ps 85:11)?
>
> B 1.3 How can a dynamic relationship of gift exchange between the churches grow?
>
> B 1.4 How can a synodal church fulfil its mission through a renewed ecumenical commitment?
>
> B 1.5 How can we recognize and gather the richness of cultures and develop dialogue amongst religions in the light of the Gospel?

### B 2. Co-responsibility in Mission: How can we better share gifts and tasks in the service of the Gospel?

---

4. Paragraphs under "Enunciation" are a–z; Arabic numerals are used for paragraphs that articulate "Prayer and Preparatory Reflection."

B 2.1 How can we walk together towards a shared awareness of the meaning and content of mission?

B 2.2 What should be done so a synodal church is also an "all ministerial" missionary church?

B 2.3 How can the church of our time better fulfil its mission through greater recognition and promotion of the baptismal dignity of women?

B 2.4 How can we properly value ordained ministry in its relationship with baptismal ministries in a missionary perspective?

B 2.5 How can we renew and promote the Bishop's ministry from a missionary synodal perspective?

**B 3. Participation, Governance and Authority. What processes, structures and institutions are needed in a missionary synodal church?**

B 3.1 How can we renew the service of authority and the exercise of responsibility in a missionary synodal church?

B 3.2 How can we develop discernment practices and decision-making processes in an authentically synodal manner, that respects the protagonism of the Spirit?

B 3.3. What structures can be developed to strengthen a missionary synodal church?

B 3.4 How can we give structure to instances of synodality and collegiality that involve groupings of local churches?

B 3.5 How can the institution of the synod be strengthened so that it is an expression of episcopal collegiality within an all-synodal church?

## B 1: A Communion That Radiates

### Enunciation

In a synodal church, the poor, that is, those living in conditions of material poverty and social exclusion, occupy a central place (1, a).

Concern also emerged that the poorest to whom the Good News is primarily addressed are too often on the margins of Christian communities (for example, migrants and refugees, street children, homeless persons, victims of human trafficking, and others) (2, d).

Caring for our common home calls for shared action and collaboration with members of other churches and ecclesial communities, with believers of other religions and with people of goodwill (1, b).

The final documents of the Continental Assemblies often mention those who do not feel accepted in the church, such as the divorced and remarried, people in polygamous marriages, or LGBTQ+ Catholics (2, a).

They also note how racial, tribal, ethnic, class or caste-based discrimination, also present in the People of God, leads some to feel less important or welcome in the community (2, b).

It is desired that we might better hear and recognize the different traditions of specific regions and churches in an ecclesial and theological conversation often dominated by Latin/Western voices (3, a).

It is desired that the Eastern Catholic Churches in the diaspora are able to preserve their identity and be recognized as more than ethnic communities, i.e., as churches *sui iuris* with rich spiritual, theological and liturgical traditions that contribute to the mission of the church today in a global context (3, c).

Through one Baptism all Christians participate in the *sensus fidei* (supernatural sense of the faith; cf. *LG*, 12), which is why in a synodal church all the baptized must be listened to attentively (4, a).

Synodality is part of the "continuous reform" of the church, as it is principally through its internal reform, in which synodality plays an essential role, that the Catholic Church draws closer to other Christians (*UR* 4.6) (4, d).

Indeed, both synodality and ecumenism are rooted in the baptismal dignity of the entire People of God. . . . They are processes of listening and dialogue and invite us to grow in a communion that is not uniformity but unity in legitimate diversity. They are spiritual processes of repentance, forgiveness, and reconciliation in a dialogue of conversion that can lead to a healing of memory (4, f).

As the Digital Synod initiative shows, the church is already present [in the digital environment and new media] through the activity of many Christians, especially the young. However, what continues to be lacking is a fuller awareness of the potential this environment offers for evangelization or a reflection, particularly in anthropological terms, on the challenges it poses (1.5).

Various tensions emerged in the work of the preparatory phase; these need not overwhelm us, but can be engaged as sources of dynamism:

> *In the relationship between the Gospel and local cultures.* Some see the adoption of the traditions of the universal church as an imposition on local cultures or even a form of colonialism. Others believe that the Spirit acts in every culture, making it already capable of giving expression to the truths of the Christian faith. Others again hold that Christians cannot adopt or adapt pre-Christian cultural practices (5, a).

> *In the relationship between Christianity and other religions.* While there are very fruitful experiences of dialogue and engagement, in some regions, difficulties, limitations, and indications of mistrust emerge, and even conflict and direct or indirect persecution (5, b).

> *In the relationship to the world.* Some forces in the world are based on philosophical, economic, and political ideologies that are founded on assumptions inimical to the faith. Not everyone perceives these tensions in the same way. Sometimes this tension is interpreted in a reductionist way as the clash between those who desire change and those who fear it (5, c).

> *In the relationship between the Christian community and young people.* Many feel excluded by the language adopted in church contexts which can seem incomprehensible to them (5, e).

## *Discernment, Prayer, and Preparatory Reflection*

How are we building a synodal church capable of promoting the belonging and participation of the least within the church and in society?

> The inequalities that mark the contemporary world are also present in the church, separating, for example, the churches of rich and poor countries and the communities of the richest and poorest areas of the same country (1, 2).

> How can welcoming migrants become an opportunity to walk with people from another culture, especially when we share the same faith? How is the Diaspora of the Eastern Catholic Churches valued and how can their presence become an opportunity to experience unity in diversity? (1, 4).

> Does the Christian community know how to accompany society as a whole in building the common good, or does it seek to defend

only its own vested interests? Is the Christian community able to bear witness to the possibility of concord beyond political polarizations? How does the community accompany its members who are engaged in politics? (1, 5).

Should the church recognize a specific ministry of listening and accompaniment for those who take on this service? (1, 7).

How can we become a church that deals honestly with its conflicts and is not afraid to safeguard spaces for disagreement? (2, 2).

How can we walk together with young people? How can a "preferential option for young people" be at the center of our pastoral strategies and synodal life? (2, 4).

How can we continue to take meaningful and concrete steps to offer justice to victims and survivors of sexual abuse and spiritual, economic, power and conscience abuse by persons who were carrying out a ministry or ecclesial responsibility? (2, 5).

In the light of the Post-Synodal Apostolic Exhortation *Amoris laetitia*, what concrete steps are needed to welcome those who feel excluded from the church because of their status or sexuality (for example, remarried divorcees, people in polygamous marriages, LGBTQ+ people, etc.)? (2, 6).

How can the local churches be helped to promote the catholicity of the church in a harmonious relationship between unity and diversity, preserving the specificity of each one? (1.3)

How can we facilitate an exchange of experiences and visions of synodality between the Eastern Catholic Churches and the Latin Church? (3, 2).

How can we take account of and value the contributions and experiences of the local churches in the teaching of the magisterium and ecclesiastical norms at the universal level? (3, 6).

How can the Oriental Catholic Churches in Diaspora preserve their identity and be recognized as more than just ethnic communities? (3, 4).

In which areas is a "healing of memory" necessary with regard to the relationship with other churches and ecclesial communities? How can we build a "new memory" together? (4, 3).

How could a common commemoration of the 1700th anniversary of the Council of Nicaea (325–2025) provide such an opportunity? (4, 4).

"The episcopal ministry of unity is closely linked to synodality." How is the bishop, as the "visible principle and foundation of unity" (*LG* 23), called to promote ecumenism in a synodal manner in his local church? (4, 5).

How can the ongoing synodal process contribute to "finding a form of exercising the primacy which, while in no way renouncing the essential nature of its mission, is open to a new situation"?[5] (4, 6).

How can we proclaim the Gospel effectively in different contexts and cultures, in order to foster the encounter with Christ for the men and women of our time? What bonds can we establish with the adherents of other religions to build a culture of encounter and dialogue (1.5).

Various dioceses, episcopal conferences, and Continental Assemblies have expressed the wish to be able to re-articulate community life and especially the liturgy in accordance with local cultures. What synodal dynamic can we put in place to meet this desire? (5, 3).

How can formation in cultural discernment be promoted? How do we foster, educate, and give recognition to the charisms and vocations of "translators," i.e., those who help build bridges between religions, cultures and people? (5, 4).

For some, secularized society is a threat to be opposed, for others a fact to be accepted, and for still others a source of inspiration and an opportunity. How can the churches remain in dialogue with the world without becoming worldly? (5, 7).

# B 2. Co-responsibility in Mission

## *Enunciation*

Synodality is constitutively missionary and mission itself is synodal action.... In the reflections of the Continental Assemblies, this mission articulates a multiplicity of dimensions that are to be harmonized and not opposed to each other in the integral perspective promoted by *Evangelii nuntiandi* and taken up by *Evangelii gaudium*.

---

5. John Paul II, *Ut Unum sint*, no. 95.

The Continental Assemblies also voice the lack of clarity and shared understanding of the meaning, scope, and content of the church's mission or the criteria for articulating its diverse expressions. Hence the demand for new modes of formation and places of encounter and dialogue, in a synodal key, between the different perspectives, spiritualities and sensitivities that make up the richness of the church (1, d).

There is a heartfelt call for the renewal of the liturgical life of the local church as a place of proclamation through Word and Sacrament, emphasizing the quality of preaching and the language of the liturgy. The latter requires a proper balance between church unity, also expressed in the unity of its rite, and legitimate diversities which a proper inculturation takes into account (1, a).

The church is discovering an opportunity for evangelization in the digital environment. It recognizes that building networks of relationships in this space makes it possible for people, especially young people, to experience new ways of walking together (1, d).

The synodal process offers a positive vision of ministries, placing ordained ministry within broader ecclesial ministeriality, without creating oppositions. However, the Continental Assemblies also note an urgent need to discern the emerging charisms and the appropriate forms of exercising baptismal ministries (instituted, extraordinary, and *de facto*) within the People of God (2.2).

There is a clear call to overcome a vision that reserves any active function in the church to ordained ministers alone (bishops, priests, deacons), reducing the participation of the baptized to a subordinated collaboration. The necessary relationship between common and ministerial priesthood is reaffirmed since they are "interrelated," each one, "in its own special way," being a "participation in the one Priesthood of Christ" (*LG* 10) (2, a).

There is a need to give new impetus and more incisive competence to the special participation of the laity in evangelization in the various spheres of social, cultural, economic and political life, assuming their own responsibilities, as well as enhancing the contribution of consecrated men and women, with their different charisms, within the life of the local church (2, b).

An all-ministerial church is not necessarily wholly a church of instituted ministries. Many ministries flow legitimately from the baptismal vocation, including spontaneous ministries and other recognized ministries that are not instituted and others that, by virtue of being instituted, receive a specific formation, mission and stability (2, d).

The desire for a greater presence of women in positions of responsibility and governance emerged as crucial elements in the search for more synodal ways to live the church's mission. A synodal church must address these questions together, seeking greater recognition of women's baptismal dignity and rejecting all forms of discrimination and exclusion faced by women in church and society (3, c).

How, in consecrated life, can women be better represented in the church's governance and decision-making processes, better protected from abuse in all ecclesial contexts, and more fairly remunerated for their work? (3, b).

The Continental Assemblies highlight the plurality of women's experiences, points of view and perspectives, and demand avoiding treating women as a homogeneous group or an abstract or ideological subject of debate (3, d).

The Continental Assemblies express a clear appreciation for priests, also a deep desire for their renewal in a synodal perspective. They also note the widespread concern for instances where priests struggle to face the challenges of our time, are far from the life and needs of the people or are focused on the liturgical-sacramental sphere only, also for the loneliness experienced by many priests, emphasizing their need for care, friendship, and support (4, b).

Also requested is a renewal of seminary programs so as to be more synodally oriented and more in contact with the whole People of God (4, c).

Many regions report that trust in ordained ministers has been undermined by the consequences of the "scandal of abuse by members of the clergy or by people holding ecclesial office. This is an open wound that continues to inflict pain on victims and survivors, on their families, and on their communities" (*DCS*, no. 20; 4, e).

To the bishops, the Continental Assemblies ask for a synodal conversion, a radical trust in the action of the Spirit in the life of their communities, without fearing that the participation of everyone need be a threat to their ministry of community leadership (5, b).

Becoming a more synodal church also implies a broader involvement of all in discernment, which requires a rethinking of decision-making processes. Consequently, there is need for adequate governance structures which respond to the demand for greater transparency and accountability. Some call for the greater involvement of all the faithful and thus a "less exclusive" exercise of the bishops' role, others express doubts and fear the risk of drift if left to the processes of political democracy (5, c).

The ministry of the bishop also includes belonging to the College of Bishops and consequently exercising co-responsibility for the whole church. This exercise is also part of the perspective of the synodal church, "in the spirit of a 'healthy decentralization,'" "to leave to the competence of bishops the authority to resolve, in the exercise of 'their proper task as teachers' and pastors, those issues with which they are familiar and that do not affect the church's unity of doctrine, discipline, and communion"[6] (5, f).

## *Discernment, Prayer, and Preparatory Reflection*

How can we move towards a meaningful and effective co-responsibility in the church, in which there is a fuller realization of the vocations, charisms, and ministries of all the baptized in a missionary key? (2.2).

How should we celebrate Baptism, Confirmation, and the Eucharist so they witness to and promote the participation and co-responsibility of all in the life and mission of the church? (2.2, 1).

How can we discern the baptismal ministries necessary for mission in a local church, whether instituted or not? What spaces are available for experimentation at the local level? (2, 2).

For the vast majority of the People of God, mission is accomplished by "engaging in temporal affairs and by ordering them according to the plan of God" (*LG* 31; cf. also *AA* 2). How can we raise awareness that professional, social, and political commitment and voluntary work are areas in which mission is exercised? (2, 4).

How can we encourage its [Church's Social Doctrine] re-appropriation by the People of God as a resource for mission? (2, 5).

What concrete steps can the church take to renew and reform its procedures, institutional arrangements and structures to enable greater recognition and participation of women, including in

---

6. *PE* II, 2; cf. *EG* 16; *DV* 7; 5, f.

## THE DOCUMENTS: INSTRUMENTUM LABORIS

governance, decision-making processes and in the taking of decisions, in a spirit of communion and with a view to mission? (2.3).

All Continental Assemblies call for the issue of women's participation in governance, decision-making, mission and ministries at all levels of the church to be addressed, and for this participation to be given the support of appropriate structures so that this does not remain just a general aspiration (3, 3).

Most of the Continental Assemblies and the syntheses of several episcopal conferences call for the question of women's inclusion in the diaconate to be considered. Is it possible to envisage this, and in what way? (3, 4).

How does the ministry of priests, "consecrated to preach the Gospel, shepherd the faithful, and celebrate divine worship" (*LG* 28), relate to baptismal ministries? (4, 1).

In the local church, priests with their bishops "constitute one priesthood" (*LG* 28). How can we help strengthen this unity between the bishop and his priests for more effective service to the People of God entrusted to the bishop's care? (4, 2).

The church is enriched by the ministry of so many priests who belong to Institutes of Consecrated Life and Societies of Apostolic Life. How can their ministry, characterized by the charism of the Institute to which they belong, promote a more synodal church? (4, 3).

What guidelines could be adopted for the reform of seminary curricula and teaching programs in colleges and schools of theology in order to promote the synodal character of the church? How can the formation of priests engage more closely with the life and pastoral realities of the People of God they are called to serve? (4, 5).

Can lay people perform the role of community leaders, particularly in places where the number of ordained ministers is very low? What implications does this have for the understanding of ordained ministry? (4, 8).

As some continents propose, could a reflection be opened concerning the discipline on access to the priesthood for married men, at least in some areas? (4, 9).

On the basis of what criteria can a bishop evaluate himself and be evaluated in the performance of his service in a synodal style? (5, 3).

What is the nature of the relationship between the "supernatural sense of the faith" (cf. *LG* 12) and the bishop's magisterial service? Should bishops discern together with or separately from the other members of the People of God? Do both options (together and separately) have a place in a synodal church? (5, 5).

How can the profile of the bishop and the discernment process be revised to identify candidates in a synodal perspective? (5, 6).

How should the role of the Bishop of Rome and the exercise of his primacy evolve in a synodal church? (5, 7).

## B 3. Participation, Governance, and Authority

*Enunciation*

Spiritual authority linked to a charism is different from that linked to ministerial service. The differences between these forms must be safeguarded, without forgetting that they all have in common the fact that they are a service in the church (1, a).

The Continental Assemblies note the fears of those who see a competition between the synodal and hierarchical dimensions that are both constitutive of the church. However, in one example, the experience of a relevant authority taking a decision within a synodal process made the community more ready to accept its legitimacy; in another, there is growing awareness that the lack of healthy exchange within a community weakens the role of authority, sometimes to a mere assertion of power. In a third, in a region where the number of priests is very low, ecclesial responsibilities have been entrusted to lay faithful who exercise them in a constructive and non-oppositional manner (2, b).

Co-responsibility in the mission deriving from Baptism must take on concrete structural forms. This should not be read as a demand for a redistribution of power. Baptism confers rights and duties on each person which each one must be able to exercise according to his or her charisms and ministries (3, a).

The Continental Assemblies expressed the conviction that structures alone are not enough, but that a change of mindset is also needed, hence the need to invest in formation (3, d).

Moreover, action in the area of canon law seems advisable: rebalancing the relationship between the principle of authority, which is strongly affirmed in the current legislation, and the principle of participation; strengthening the synodal orientation of already existing institutions; creating new institutions, where this appears necessary for the needs of community life; supervising the effective application of current legislation (3, e).

"We need to reflect on how better to bring about, through these bodies, intermediary instances of collegiality, perhaps by integrating and updating certain aspects of the ancient ecclesiastical organization."[7]

## *Discernment, Prayer, and Preparatory Reflection*

In the church there are roles of authority and responsibility, not linked to the Sacrament of Orders, which are exercised at the service of communion and mission in Institutes of Consecrated Life and Societies of Apostolic Life. How can these forms of authority be appropriately promoted and how can they be exercised in relationship with the ministerial authority of the pastors within a synodal church? (1, 2).

How can and must consecrated men and women participate in the decision-making processes of the local churches? What can we learn from their experience and their different spiritualities regarding discernment and decision-making processes? What can we learn from associations, movements, and lay-led groups? (2, 6).

How should the *Ratio Fundamentalis Institutionis Sacerdotalis* and its related documents be rethought at the national level? How should curricula in theology schools be reoriented? (1, 4).

To what extent does the shortage of priests in some regions provide an incentive to question the relationship between ordained ministry, governance, and the assumption of responsibilities in the Christian community? (1, 6).

How can Conversation in the Spirit contribute to the renewal of decision-making processes in the church? What changes in canon law are needed to facilitate this? (2, 2).

How can we promote the ministry of the facilitator of community discernment processes, ensuring that those who carry it out receive adequate formation and accompaniment? (3.2, 3).

---

7. Francis, "Address on 50th Anniversary," no. 18.

How can we deal constructively with cases in which those in authority feel they cannot confirm the conclusions reached by a community discernment process, taking a decision in a different direction? (2, 7; see B 2.5.4).

How should canonical structures and pastoral procedures change to foster co-responsibility and transparency? Are the structures we have adequate to ensure participation or do we need new ones? (3, 1).

How can canon law contribute to the renewal of structures and institutions? What changes seem necessary or opportune? (3, 2).

What degree of doctrinal authority can be attributed to the discernment of episcopal conferences? How do the Eastern Catholic Churches regulate their episcopal bodies? (4, a)?

What degree of doctrinal authority can be attributed to the discernment of a Continental Assembly? Or of the bodies that bring together episcopal conferences on a continental or otherwise international scale? (b);

Which role does the Bishop of Rome fulfil in regard of these processes involving groupings of churches? In which ways can he exercise it? (4, c).

The Second Vatican Council states that the whole church and all its parts benefit from the mutual sharing of their respective gifts (cf. *LG* 13) (4):

What value can the deliberations of a Plenary Council, a Particular Council, a Diocesan Synod have for other churches? (4, a).

What insights can the Latin Church draw from the rich synodal experience of the Eastern Catholic Churches? (4, b).

How is the service of unity entrusted to the Bishop of Rome to be exercised when local institutions may adopt different approaches? What room is there for a variety of approaches between different regions? (4, d).

In light of the dynamic and reciprocal relationship between the church's synodality, episcopal collegiality, and Petrine primacy, how should the institution of the synod be perfected so that it becomes a secure and guaranteed space for the exercise of synodality that ensures the full participation of all—the People of God, the College of Bishops and the Bishop of Rome—while respecting their specific functions? How should we evaluate the experiment of extending participation to a group of non-bishops in the first session of the XVI Ordinary General Assembly of the Synod of Bishops (October 2023)? (3.5).

How can the Eastern Hierarchical Structures, Episcopal Conferences, and Continental Assemblies strengthen the "fruitful bond between the *sensus fidei* of the People of God and the magisterial function of the pastors" (*PD* 14)? (5, b).

How desirable is the presence of qualified members of the People of God in the assemblies of the episcopal conferences as well as in the Continental Assemblies? (5, c).

What role might be played by ecclesial bodies permanently composed of more than just bishops, such as the recently established Ecclesial Conference for the Amazon Region? (5, d).

## BRIEF REVIEW OF THE *INSTRUMENTUM LABORIS*

Cardinal Jean-Claude Hollerich, the Synod Relator, in a June 30, 2023 interview with the journalist Gerard O'Connell asserted that "this is not Vatican III, as some people say. This is going back to Vatican II seriously, trying to implement Vatican II."[8] In fact, the same journalist later put it this way: "The synod is not Vatican III. It's Pope Francis' implementation of Vatican II."[9] The *IL*, while faithfully reporting on the consultations, embedded them within Pope Francis' theology and spirituality: of the fifteen citations in *IL*, ten cite works or Addresses of Pope Francis.

*IL* centers the harmony of unity and diversity in the church in *perichōrēsis*, the unity and diversity in the Trinity. A synodal church is a church of "mutual empowerment" in which all charisms and gifts function together for mission, hence co-responsibility at all levels.

Mission is redefined. "Communion and mission interpenetrate and mutually imply each other" (*IL*, Theological Introduction, no. 44). Baptism is the new basis for articulating anew the meaning, scope, and content of the church's mission or the criteria for its diverse expressions (B 2.1, d). The multiplicity of dimensions of mission are to be harmonized in the integral perspective promoted especially by *Evangelii nuntiandi* and taken up in *Evangelium gaudium* (B 2.1).

---

8. O'Connell, "Cardinal Hollerich: 'Synod Is Not.'"
9. O'Connell, "Analysis: Synod Is Not."

*DCS* no. 64 noted that "much greater diversity of opinion was expressed on the subject of priestly ordination for women, which some reports call for, while others consider a closed issue." The *Instrumentum laboris* (Worksheet B 2.34) passes this over in silence to focus on the diaconate, writing that "most of the Continental Assemblies and the syntheses of several episcopal conferences call for the question of women's inclusion in the diaconate to be considered."

The dialectic of "love and truth" (Ps 85:11, "love and truth will meet"; Eph 5:15–16, "speaking the truth in love") refers to "the Christological paradox of boldly proclaiming its authentic teaching while at the same time offering a witness of radical inclusion and acceptance through its pastoral and discerning accompaniment (*DCS*, no. 30). This enshrines Pope Francis' pastoral practice and saw animated discussion at the October 2023 synod assembly.

# 6

# Discordant Voices on the Synod on Synodality

## THE GERMAN SYNODAL WAY

EVEN BEFORE POPE FRANCIS launched the Synod on Synodality the German Episcopal Conference at Lingen, on December 1, 2019, as a response to the clergy sexual abuse, approved a "Synodal Way" (*Synodaler Weg*) originally intended to last two years, until 2021. It would be a permanent and deliberative synodal council of clergy and laity, a supra-diocesan body for pastoral planning and budgetary matters.

The Vatican vetoed the idea of a council placed over and above the bishops, the official pastors of the church. On April 11, 2022, 103 prelates worldwide wrote a letter of caution to the German Episcopal Conference.[1] On January 16, 2023, Cardinals Parolin, Marc Ouellet, and Luis Ladaria equally wrote to Bishop Georg Bätzing, president of the German Episcopal Conference since March 2020:

> The "Synodal Council" would constitute a new governance structure for the church in Germany, which . . . appears to stand above the authority of the German Bishops' Conference and, in fact

---

1. The authors included Cardinal Burke (USA), Cardinal Arinze (Nigeria), Cardinal Napier (South Africa), Cardinal Pell (Australia), Cardinal Ruini (Italy), and Cardinal Zen (Hong Kong). See Arinze et al., "Fraternal Open Letter."

replace it . . . Neither the Synodal Way, anybody established by it, nor any bishop's conference has the competence to establish a Synodal Council at the national, diocesan, or parish levels.[2]

A bishop presides over each of the four forums (power, participation, and separation of powers; sexual morals; form of priestly life; and women in the services and offices of the church), but the voting is strictly egalitarian.[3] On power in the church, it is held that "the access of married priests and women to these ministries, including the ordained ministry, must be openly debated."[4] For genuine participation, "effective procedures in a clear separation of powers should be introduced for all forms of the exercise of power by the church . . . Specifically, this means that the direction, legislation, and jurisdiction of the church not be solely in the hands of the bishop . . . All the People of God must be involved in legislation."[5] Nearly 80 percent (168 of 214 delegates) voted for further discussion and "re-examination" of the church's teaching on sexual morality and included a call for the liturgical blessings of same-sex couples.

In the summer of 2019, Pope Francis had written to the Church in Germany warning against the temptation "to get out of its problems alone, relying solely on its own strengths, methods, and intelligence." This can end up, "multiplying and nurturing the evils it wanted to overcome."[6] On January 25, 2023 in an interview the pope further said, "The German experience does not help . . . the danger is that something very, very ideological will enter. When ideology gets involved in church processes, the Holy Spirit goes home because ideology overcomes the Holy Spirit."[7]

Concerned world church leaders began to speak of German schism. Cardinal Marx, the leader of the German Church, sent in his resignation; Pope Francis turned it down. After the CDF declaration, approved by Pope Francis, that "God does not and cannot bless sin," and that "gay people must be treated with dignity and respect, but that gay sex is 'intrinsically disordered,'" many pastors in Germany chose one day to simultaneously bless same-sex couples.

2. Allen, "Vatican, German Bishops," §§11, 13.
3. FSSPX News, "Synodal Path."
4. FSSPX News, "Synodal Path," §28.
5. FSSPX News, "Synodal Path," §25.
6. Dulle, "German Synodal Way, Explained."
7. Cernuzio, "Il Papa," Qs. 89.

In a letter published in *Die Welt* on November 21, 2023, but dated a day earlier, Pope Francis wrote: "'I also share in this concern over the numerous concrete steps that are taking place.'" He wrote that parts of the German Church are "'threatening to move even further away from the common path of our universal church.'" The same day, "the Synodal Path participants approved the creation of a synodal committee, composed of bishops and lay delegates," which would be responsible for creating the Permanent Synodal Council by 2026. "Francis explicitly wrote that the synodal committee, 'as outlined in the corresponding resolution, is not in alignment with the sacramental structure of the Catholic Church.'"[8]

## THE SYNOD PROCESS IS A PANDORA'S BOX

A book of this title consisting of a hundred questions and answers was published before the *IL* was presented on June 20, 2023; a postface was tagged on thereafter. The authors, who sent it to 41,000 bishops, priests, deacons, and religious in the USA, belong to the American Society for the Defense of Tradition, Family, and Property, a conservative group that advocates unfettered capitalism. Cardinal Burke wrote in the Foreword about:

> synodality, a term which has no history in the doctrine of the church and for which there is no reasonable definition. Synodality and its adjective, synodal, have become slogans behind which a revolution is at work to change radically the church's self-understanding.

In the Introduction the authors assert that:

> A maneuver is underway to demolish Holy Mother Church by erasing the basic elements of her organic constitution and doctrine, rendering her unrecognizable.[9]

The equal dignity of all the baptized, the new valuation of lay charisms and ministries, and Pope Francis' emphasis on an "inverted pyramid" threaten the hierarchical structure of *ecclesia docens* over against *ecclesia discerns* (Qs. 43). Attention to experience and listening to the People of God stand in the way of truths of faith known through Revelation and Tradition and applied to concrete life. "Radical inclusion" is being "applied to

---

8. Giangravé, "Pope Francis Warns German Synodal Path," §§2, 6, 7.

9. Ureta and de Izcue, *Synodal Process Is a Pandora's Box*. I worked from an online copy with no page numbers, so I cite the question number.

overturn all the church dogmatic and ethical teaching" (Qs. 31). Women now want to be ordained deacons and priests, homosexuals and bi-sexual people want acceptance without conversion, lay people want the authority given by God to bishops and priests (Qs. 33). The term *process* occurs no less than twenty-three times in *DCS*, along with the synonyms *path, route, itinerary*. "Francis privileges becoming not being, change not stability, search not certainty" (Qs. 7). Timothy Radcliffe, invited as preacher for the spiritual retreat of the synod, "is known for his heterodox positions and, above all, for his activism in favor of recognizing homosexuality within the church" (Qs. 96). The *IL* just issued "increases the perplexities and concerns." From the beginning the clear intention is to make synodality a "constitutive dimension" of the church.

## BISHOP ATHANASIUS SCHNEIDER

Bishop Schneider is the Auxiliary Bishop of Astana in Kazakhstan. On June 29, 2023, upon the publication of the *IL*, he published an abrasive "appeal for prayer and reflection."[10]

"Immorality regarding marriage is implicitly promoted when the document laments those 'who do not feel accepted in the church, such as the divorced and remarried, people in polygamous marriages'" (B 1.2, a). The *so-called LGBTQ movement is implicitly promoted*, which includes promoting homosexual activity and the current worldwide totalitarian 'gender ideology.'" The so-called "Conversation in the Spirit" (nos. 32–42) is a "*subjectivistic 'pentecostalization' of the life* of the church by presumably attributing to human dialogue, non-official prayers, and mutual exchange of views a vague spiritual quality." Among grave omissions: "absence of a discussion of Eucharistic adoration, the Cross of Christ, and man's final end in eternity."

The *IL* "appears to undermine the divine constitution and the Apostolic character of the life and mission of the church"; it is "inspired predominantly by Protestant, social, and anthropocentric categories." Demanding "greater involvement of all the faithful" and thus a "less exclusive" exercise of the bishops' role (B 2.5, c) undermines episcopal authority. The ambiguous use of "ministry" in the phrase "to foster an understanding of ministries that is not reduced to ordained ministry" (B 3.4) undermines the hierarchical structure of the church. So also does the call for women's participation

---

10. Schneider, "New 'Synodal Church,'" §§9–10, 13, 15.

in governance, decision-making, mission and ministries at all levels of the church (B 2.3.3). The unity of the sacrament of Holy Order is undermined by the "call" for the question of women's inclusion in the diaconate to be considered (B 2.3.4). The *IL* substitutes for "the One, Holy, Catholic and Apostolic Church a fantasy 'synodal church' that is worldly, bureaucratic, anthropocentric, neo-Pelagian, and hierarchically and doctrinally vague. But we do not believe in—nor would anyone give his life for—a 'synodal church.'"[11]

## GEORGE WEIGEL

His summary judgment is: "There is much in the church in need of renewal and reform. The [*IL*] for the Synod on Synodality does not advance that cause. Nor does it reflect the Christocentric teaching and spirit of Vatican II." His operational term is "vacuous"—Christologically vacuous, pneumatologically vacuous, ecclesiologically vacuous. Besides, it is "woefully lacking in moral theology" and "methodologically childish."[12] His response calls forth William Shakespeare, *Hamlet*, Act 3, Scene 2, line 253: "Methinks, the lady doth protest too much."

## CARDINAL JOSEPH ZEN ZE-KIUN

Cardinal Zen, ninety-one years old and from Hong Kong, addressed himself directly to the Cardinals and Excellencies of the Synod. They should be as worried as he is about the outcome of this synod. "Synodality is . . . a new term; from its etymology we can understand that it is a matter of a certain spirit of 'conversing together and walking together.'" "The novelty of the term 'synodality' demands a careful assessment of its theological significance." If it is said that synodality is a constitutive element of the church, "How can God have forgotten to make his church live out this constitutive element in the 20 centuries of her existence?"[13]

Without consultation, just when the synod was about to begin, the Holy Father added a number of lay members with right of vote. This

---

11. Schneider, "New 'Synodal Church,'" §§1, 2, 5, 7, 18–19.

12. Weigel, "Laborious and Vacuous Instrument," §§8–9. Weigel is a senior fellow at the Ethics and Public Policy Center, Washington, DC, where he holds the William E. Simon Chair in Catholic Studies.

13. Wimmer, "Cardinal Zen Expresses Concerns."

radically changes the nature of the synod, which Paul VI intended as instrument of episcopal collegiality (even if lay "observers" were generally admitted). He suggests protesting to let the votes of the bishops and the votes of the lay people be counted separately. Are they sure that these lay people are *fideles*, that at least they still go to church? "As a matter of fact, these lay people have not been elected by the Christian people." "There has been no explanation for the addition (halfway through) of another synodal session for 2024." My malicious suspicion is that "the organizers, not sure to be able to reach during this session their goals, are opting for more time to maneuver."[14]

The suggestion is made that the day has come to "overturn the pyramid,[15] that is, with the hierarchy surmounted by the lay people." "The Synod Secretariat is very efficient at the art of manipulation. They begin by saying that we must listen to all. Little by little they make us understand that among these 'all' there are especially those whom we have 'excluded.' Finally, we understand that what they mean are people who opt for a sexual morality different than of Catholic tradition . . . Often they claim not to have any agenda . . . Anybody can see which conclusions they are aiming at." They want only "conversation in the Spirit." "Conversation, no discussion! Discussions create divisions!" "You must not obey them, when they tell you to go and pray . . . Tell them that it is ridiculous to think that the Holy Spirit is waiting for these your prayers offered at the last moment."[16]

---

14. Wimmer, "Cardinal Zen Expresses Concerns."

15. For record purposes, what Pope Francis ("Ceremony for the 50th Anniversary") said was, "But in this church, as in an inverted pyramid, the top is located below the base. Consequently, those who exercise authority are called 'ministers,' because, in the original meaning of the word, they are the least of all."

16. Wimmer, "Cardinal Zen Expresses Concerns."

# 7

# Participation in the Synod 2023 Session

ON APRIL 26, 2023, the Secretariat for the Synod announced that seventy "non-bishop members" appointed by the pope—half of whom will be women—would be able to vote at the General Assembly of the Synod in October. "The changes were presented by Cardinal Mario Grech, Secretary General of the Secretariat for the Synod, and Cardinal Jean-Claude Hollerich, the Synod's General Relator." They state that "no current regulations have been repealed, and that the 2018 Apostolic Constitution *Episcopalis communio* already provided for the presence of 'non-bishops' at the Synod."[1]

The assembly consisted of 464 persons. Bishops' Conferences and Oriental Churches with over a hundred members[2] elected four bishops; those with fewer than twenty-five elected one bishop. The pope personally nominated 120 attendees (bishops, religious, and laity) of which fifty-two were delegates. Bishops attending the synod were 79 percent of the assembly. The seventy-five non-voting participants included experts, special assistants, and twenty-six (priest) facilitators, two of whom were Africans.

For the first time in the synod process, the lay faithful (religious and laity) were invited as members with right of vote. Of the 346 with right to vote, seventy were lay faithful (of whom fifty-four were women).[3]

---

1. Cernuzio, "Synod: Laymen and Laywomen."

2. Among them are the USA, Canada, France, Italy, Brazil, Mexico, the Democratic Republic of the Congo, India.

3. There is some discrepancy in the figures. The actual voting record has 344 from the Introduction through part 1 of the *Synthesis Report*, but 346 from part 2 through the Conclusion.

There were thirty priests among those with right to vote.[4] However, none was a pastor. This gaping omission was remedied as three hundred of them, chosen according to the criteria used for bishops, met in Fraterna Domus in Sacrofano, near Rome from Sunday, April 29 to Thursday, May 2, 2024.

Pope Francis is the president of the Assembly, Cardinal Jean-Claude Hollerich, SJ, Archbishop of Luxembourg, the General Relator. All heads of the Roman dicasteries were invited. Retreat preachers and spiritual assistants were: Father Timothy Peter Joseph Radcliffe, OP (Oxford, England) and Mother Maria Ignazia Angelini, OSB (Monastery of Viboldone, Italy). In the assemblies, Professor Anna Rowlands, theologian of Catholic social thought and practice, Durham University (UK), joined Fr. Radcliffe to give theological reflections on the Modules.

The USA bishops whom Pope Francis nominated included allies, Cardinal Blase Cupich (Archbishop of Chicago); Cardinal Wilton Gregory (Archbishop of Washington, DC); and Cardinal Robert Walter McElroy (Bishop of San Diego).

Surprisingly, the pope nominated his critic, Cardinal Gerhard Ludwig Müller (Prefect Emeritus, Congregation for Doctrine of the Faith), but Cardinal Raymond Burke was beyond the pale. Bishop Georg Bätzing of Limburg, who presides over the German Synodal Way, was one of the three elected by the German Episcopal Conference. And Thomas Söding, the vice president of the Central Committee for German Catholics (ZdK), served as a theological expert at the synod.

The nomination of Father James Martin, SJ (USA, known for LGBTQ ministry) was bold, but expected. That of Father Antonio Spadaro, SJ (director of *La Civiltà Cattolica*, Italy) and Austen Ivereigh (Oxford, Great Britain) was expected.[5]

The Commission for the *Synthesis Report* consisted of thirteen members—seven elected by the synod assembly on October 9, three personally appointed by the pope, and three de facto members from the Secretariat of the Synod. Appointed by Pope Francis: Cardinal Giorgio Marengo, IMC (Mongolia); Sister Patricia Murray, IBVM (Ireland); Father Giuseppe Bonfrate (Italy, Gregorian University, Rome).

---

4. Asia/Cambodia, 6; Italy, 5; Eastern Churches, 5; Africa, 4; France, 3; Spain, 2; USIG, 2; L. America, 1; USA, 1; Germany, 1.

5. These two have published works on Pope Francis.

Elected by the assembly were: Cardinal Fridolin Ambongo Besunu, OFMCap (Archbishop of Kinshasa); Cardinal Jean-Marc Aveline (Archbishop of Marseille); Cardinal Gérald Cyprien Lacroix, ISPX (served as Archbishop of Quebec, named early 2023 to the pope's Council of Cardinals); Bishop Shane Anthony Mackinlay (served as the bishop of Sandhurst, Australia); Archbishop José Luis Azuaje Ayala (Venezuela); Bishop Mounir Khairallah (Maronite, Lebanon); Father Clarence Sandanaraj Davedassan (Malaysia).

The Vatican announced a confidentiality requirement, "In order to guarantee the freedom of expression of each and all regarding their thoughts and to ensure the serenity of the discernment in common, which is the main task entrusted to the assembly." Communication about what takes place in the synod hall will be managed by the "Commission on Information," whose report, however, will not disclose who is sitting with whom nor differentiate between votes cast by bishops and non-bishops. Synod rules forbade participants "from recording, filming, or disclosing their interventions in the synod's General Congregations and in the Working Groups."[6] An official audiovisual recording of the General Congregations will be kept in the archives of the General Secretariat of the Synod.[7] The confidentiality indeed proved liberating. Emerging tensions were handled in a synodal manner, without the exacerbation of media pressure.

---

6. Mares, "Secrecy at the Synod on Synodality."

7. In fact, they are already available at www.synod.va.

# 8

# The *Dubia* Cardinals and the Pope's Response

FIVE CARDINALS[1] IN JULY 2023 sent Pope Francis questions for clarification, called *Dubia* (*Doubts*). He ignored them. They sent them again on August 23. When they still received no reply, they made the questions public on October 2, the day before the retreat of the Synod. Pope Francis made his reply public the same day to clear the air.

The first question asked whether divine revelation should be reinterpreted based on current cultural and anthropological changes. The second concerns blessing of same-sex unions, citing canon 2357 and Rom 1:24–32 to the effect that denying sexual difference is the consequence of denying the Creator. The third questioned whether synodality is a "constitutive dimension of the church, such that the church is by nature synodal."[2] For the fourth, they cited the view of some pastors and theologians that the theology of the church and the meaning of the Mass has changed and so the sacramental ordination of women can be conferred. Finally, they whether forgiveness is a human right that he should insist on absolving everyone always, without repentance as a necessary condition for sacramental absolution.

The pope wrote in Spanish. I work from an "unofficial working translation" available online. He answered the first question as follows. If

---

1. Cardinals Walter Brandmüller and Raymond Leo Burke, supported by three other cardinals, Juan Sandoval Íñiguez, Robert Sarah, and Joseph Zen Ze-kiun.

2. *Vatican News*, "Pope Francis Responds." Unless otherwise noted, all the following quotes are from this source.

"re-interpret" is understood as "interpret better," the expression is valid. The judgment of the church may mature (*DV*, 12). Cultural changes and new challenges can stimulate us to express certain aspects of revelation better. For example, Exod 21:20–21 and Pope Nicholas V (Bull *Dum diversans*, 1452) approved slavery. Parts of the New Testament, for example, 1 Cor 11:3–10; 1 Tim 2:11–14, cannot be materially repeated today.

As to the second question, only the union of man and woman can be called "marriage." Marriage has a unique essential constitution that requires an exclusive name. However, in our relations with people, the defense of objective truth is not the only expression of pastoral charity; it also includes kindness, patience, understanding, tenderness, and encouragement. There may be forms of blessing, requested by one or more persons, that do not convey a mistaken concept of marriage. Pastoral charity requires us not to simply treat as "sinners" other people whose guilt or responsibility may be mitigated by various factors affecting subjective accountability.[3]

On the third, the church is a "mystery of missionary communion," which is not only affective or ethereal, but implies real participation. Not only the hierarchy but the entire People of God in various ways and at different levels can make their voices heard and feel part of the church's journey. In this sense, we can say that synodality, as a style and dynamism, is an essential dimension of the church's life.

On the ordination of women, when John Paul II taught that we must "definitively" affirm the impossibility of conferring priestly ordination on women, he was in no way denigrating women and giving supreme power to men; "we are in the realm of function, not of dignity and holiness."[4] Anyway, let us recognize that a clear and authoritative doctrine on the exact nature of a "definitive statement" has not yet been fully developed. It is not a dogmatic definition, and yet it must be adhered to by all. No one can publicly contradict it and yet it can be a subject of study, as with the case of the validity of ordinations in the Anglican Communion.

Finally, repentance is necessary for the validity of sacramental absolution and implies a resolution not to sin. But the confessional is not a customs house. We are not masters, rather humble stewards of the sacraments. More than relics to be preserved, they are aids of the Holy Spirit for people's lives. There are many ways to express repentance. Sometimes, the very act of approaching the confessional is a symbolic expression of repentance and

---

3. See John Paul II, *Reconciliatio et paenitentia*, 17.
4. John Paul II, *Christifideles laici*, no. 190.

of seeking divine help. Note also that all the conditions usually attached to confession are generally not applicable when a person is in a situation of agony, or with very limited mental and psychological capacities.

# 9

# The Opening Retreat

THE SYNOD BEGAN WITH a three-day retreat for participants, thus manifesting it as a spiritual journey, not a parliamentary gathering. Fr. Radcliffe, OP, a former general of the Dominicans, opened the synod with six sessions (two meditations each day) at the *Fraterna Domus* in Rome from October 1 to October 3, 2023.

The first session, "Hoping against Hope," acknowledged the mixed feelings: "We have contradictory hopes! So how can we hope together?" He noted that "even the differences between Dominicans and Jesuits pale into insignificance" compared with the divided hopes of traditionalists and progressives! "The greatest gifts will come from those with whom we disagree, if we dare to listen to them. . . . Our hope is Eucharistic . . . We are united in the hope of the Eucharist, a hope which embraces and transcends all that we long for."[1]

The second session was titled "At Home in God and God at Home in Us."

> We need to renew the church as our common home if we are to speak to a world which is suffering from a crisis of homelessness. . . . Everywhere there is a terrible spiritual homelessness. . . . Different understandings of the church as home tear us apart today. . . . For some the idea of a universal welcome, in which everyone is accepted regardless of who they are, is felt as destructive of the church's identity. . . . They believe that identity demands

---

1. Radcliffe, "1 October 2023: First Meditation."

> boundaries. But for others, it is the very heart of the church's identity to *be* open. . . . For some of us, the Christian identity is above all given, the church we know and love. For others Christian identity is always provisional, lying ahead as we journey towards the Kingdom in which all walls will fall. Both are necessary! . . . All theology springs from tension, which bends the bow to shoot the arrow.[2]

The third was "On the Meaning of Friendship."

> This Synod will be fruitful if it leads us into a deeper friendship with the Lord and with each other. . . . St. Martin de Porres is often shown with a cat, a dog, and a mouse eating from the same dish. A good image of religious life! . . . So, we preach the gospel by friendships that reach across boundaries. . . . In the synod, we have the creative task of making improbable friendships . . . . If you think that I am talking nonsense, come and befriend me! . . . The bravest thing we can do in this synod is to be truthful about our doubts and questions with each other, the questions to which we have no clear answers. Then we shall draw near as fellow searchers, beggars for the truth.[3]

The fourth was "On the Meaning of the Conversation on the Way to Emmaus."

> Our world is filled with anger. We speak of the politics of anger. . . . This anger infects our church too. A justified anger at the sexual abuse of children. Anger at the position of women in the church. Anger at those awful conservatives or horrible liberals. Do we, like Jesus, dare to ask each other: "What are you talking about? Why are you angry?" Do we dare to hear the reply? . . . We are here to listen to the Lord, and to each other. As they say, we have two ears but only one mouth! Only after listening comes speech. . . . Notice that Jesus does not attempt to control the conversation. He asks what *they* are talking about; he goes where *they* go, not where he wishes to go; he accepts *their* hospitality. A real conversation cannot be controlled. One surrenders oneself to its direction. We cannot anticipate where it will take us, to Emmaus or Jerusalem. Where will this synod lead the church? If we knew in advance, there would be no point in having it! Let us be surprised![4]

---

2. Radcliffe, "1 October 2023: Second Meditation."
3. Radcliffe, "2 October 2023: First Meditation."
4. Radcliffe, "2 October 2023: Second Meditation."

The fifth was on "Authority."

> An Asian archbishop complained that he had no authority: "The priests are all independent barons, who take no notice of me." Many priests too say they lost all authority. The sexual abuse crisis has discredited us. . . . So how may the church recover authority and speak to our world which hungers for voices that ring true? . . . What I would suggest this morning is that authority is multiple and mutually enhancing. There need be no competition, as if the laity can only have more authority if the bishops have less, or so-called conservatives compete for authority with progressives. . . . But in the Trinity, there is no rivalry. . . . We shall speak with authority to our lost world if in this synod we transcend competitive ways of existing. . . . We shall only have authority in our fearful world if we are seen to risk everything. . . . Jonathan Sacks . . . wrote, "In turbulent times, there is an almost overwhelming temptation for religious leaders to be confrontational. Not only must truth be proclaimed but falsehood must be denounced . . . [but] a prophet hears not one imperative but two: guidance and compassion, a love of truth and an abiding solidarity with those for whom that truth has become eclipsed. To preserve tradition and at the same time defend those others condemn is the difficult, necessary task of religious leadership in an unreligious age." *If the church becomes truly a community of mutual empowerment, we shall speak with the authority of the Lord.*[5]

**Fr. Timothy Radcliffe, OP, preacher of the synod retreat**

---

5. Radcliffe, "3 October 2023: First Meditation" (italics original). I adopted *"community of mutual empowerment"* as part of the title of this work.

The final session was on "The Spirit of Truth."

> During the next three weeks, we may be tempted to call down fire from heaven on those with whom we disagree! . . . We must seek ways to speak the truth so that the other person can hear it without feeling demolished. . . . The Holy Spirit sometimes kicks us out of the nest and bids us fly! We flap in panic, but fly we will! In Gethsemane, Jesus surrenders control over his life and entrusts it to the Father. Not as I will! . . . Imagine the joy of being liberated from all competition with each other so that the more voice the laity have does not mean that the bishops have less, or the more that women are granted authority does not mean that the men have less, or the more recognition that our African brothers and sisters receive does not diminish the authority of the Church in Asia or the West. . . . If we let ourselves be guided by the Spirit of truth, we shall doubtless argue. It will sometimes be painful. There will be truths we would rather not face. But we shall be led a little deeper into the mystery of divine love and we shall know such joy that people will be envious of us for being here, and will long to attend the next session of the synod![6]

---

6. Radcliffe, "3 October 2023: Second Meditation."

# 10

# The Synod Assembly

## INNOVATIONS THAT CHARACTERIZED THE SPIRIT OF THIS SYNOD

The seating arrangement concretized what synodality meant: the People of God, in the variety of gifts and charisms, conversing together and mutually sharing the concern of church and mission. Each of the thirty-five tables (twelve persons per table, including an assigned facilitator) had cardinals, bishops, religious (men/women), and laity. Even the pope himself sat at a round table surrounded by all ranks in the church! Each person received the same time allotment to speak (three minutes). The facilitators faithfully executed their task. In one case, a facilitator had to interject, "Your Eminence, she hasn't finished yet!"

From the second week, people sat according to language groups dealing with specific topics they earlier indicated interest in.

The *Synthesis Report* described the seating arrangement as:

> emblematic of a synodal way of being church and an image of the Eucharist, which is the source and summit of synodality, with the Word of God at the center. In a church that is living synodally, different cultures, languages, rites, ways of thinking, and realities can engage together and fruitfully in a sincere search for the Spirit's guidance (1, c).

Many people would later point to this seating arrangement as the best fruit of the synod, and that synodality will go a long way if bishops adopted it in the various particular churches.

Tied to the above is "conversation in the Spirit," called the "synodal method," and the decision to begin with small groups (*circuli minores*). The necessary listening to others before speaking, and the breaks for prayer highlight spiritual discernment in common. The goal is not using all arts of rhetoric to prevail, but together listening to the Holy Spirit for the good of church and world.

**Pope Francis at his synod round table**

Until this synod, the normal thing had been to begin with plenary assemblies in which each bishop who wished might speak for eight minutes. The Relator summarized the result in a long speech. Then followed the *circuli minores*, language groupings to develop proposals for voting.

For the first time, the *IL* did not look only for consensus, but freely registered points of convergence, tensions, and matters for deeper study. That meant that everyone's views could taken into consideration. There was no need to try to suppress points of view one did not like, even if one considered them bad for the church.

## INAUGURATION MASS: HOMILY BY POPE FRANCIS

Pope Francis, in his Homily at the Inauguration Mass in St. Peter's Square, October 4, reminded the assembly of the need to be open to the Spirit.

> Brothers and sisters, holy People of God, in the face of the difficulties and challenges that lie ahead, the blessing and welcoming gaze of Jesus prevents us from falling into some dangerous temptations: of being a rigid church—a customs post—which arms itself against the world and looks backward; of being a lukewarm church, which surrenders to the fashions of the world; of being a tired church, turned in on itself. Let us continue to remember that it is not a political gathering, but a convocation in the Spirit; not a polarized parliament, but a place of grace and communion. The Holy Spirit often shatters our expectations to create something new that surpasses our predictions and negativity.[1]

## OPENING ADDRESS OF POPE FRANCIS

In his address in the Paul VI Audience Hall, Pope Francis explained that in the consultation for this synod, priests came first as priority, then synodality, the third being a social issue. "A synod is a journey that the Holy Spirit makes. You have been given a few patristic texts that can help us in the opening of the synod. They are taken from Saint Basil, who wrote that fine treatise on the Holy Spirit."[2] He continued:

> The Holy Spirit sets off a profound and varied process within the church community: the "commotion" of Pentecost . . . And after this came the great work of the Holy Spirit: not unity, no, but harmony. The Spirit unites us in harmony, the harmony of differences. If there is no harmony, the Spirit is not there . . . Harmony—we need be careful—does not mean "synthesis," but "a bond of communion between dissimilar parts." If, in this synod, we end up with an identical statement, everybody the same, without nuances, the Spirit is not there, he is left out.[3]

He pleaded with journalists to bear with the gag order on the press and the confidentiality commitment of participants. "The church is taking

---

1. Francis, "Holy Mass," no. 3.
2. Francis, "Opening of the Works," 2.
3. Francis, "Opening of the Works," 2.

a break . . . behind closed doors . . . It is a break for the whole church, as we engage in listening."[4]

## PATRISTIC TEXTS ON THE HOLY SPIRIT

These texts were proposed by Pope Francis, testimony to his belief that, with the Holy Spirit as protagonist, the synod will succeed in renewing the church. The church is a single harmony of many voices brought about by the Holy Spirit. Harmony does not mean a summation but rather the bond of communion between dissimilar parts.

The Holy Spirit is the one who makes us church. When can we judge a conversation as chatter? (Basil, *Bapt* I, 3; PG 31, 1577BC). Every word that does not contribute to the fulfilment of the Lord's will is useless. The danger of such words is so great that, no matter whatever it can be, if it is not ordered to the edification of the faith (cf. Eph 4:29), the one who spoke does not escape the danger because that word is good, but grieves the Holy Spirit because what he says is not ordered to the edification.[5]

## FIRST GENERAL CONGREGATION: WEDNESDAY, OCTOBER 4

The delegate president, Ibrahim I. Sedrak, Coptic Patriarch of Alexandria, greeted the assembly. He confessed that at the beginning of the journey many felt quite disoriented because of the newness of the modality of this synod. However, we are rediscovering the importance of journeying, listening, and discerning together what the Spirit is saying to us.

In his intervention, the Cardinal Secretary of the Synod of Bishops, Cardinal Mario Grech, asserted that the church today finds herself at a crossroads, confronting the urgent challenge of becoming a sign and instrument of the love of God for every man and woman today. More than anywhere, what John Chrysostom said has become true: "Church and Synod are synonyms" (*Explanations* in Ps. 149, PG 55, 493).

The Relator General, Jean-Claude Cardinal Hollerich, presenting his report, said:

---

4. Francis, "Opening of the Works," 4.
5. Synod of Bishops, "Collection of Patristic Texts."

We are not sitting in hierarchical order but at round tables, which is a way to foster genuine sharing and authentic discernment. The aula is not arranged in this way for practical reasons or because of a decision by the Secretariat of the Synod. It mirrors the experience of the People of God along the synodal path that started in 2021 . . . Round tables also remind us that none of us is a star in this synod. The protagonist is the Holy Spirit, and only with a heart fully open to the Spirit's guidance will we be able to respond to the call we have received as synod members.

**Cardinal Jean-Claude Hollerich, SJ, Relator of the Synod**

We are called to learn the grammar of synodality. Just like the grammar of our languages changes as they develop, so does the grammar of synodality: it changes with time. Therefore, the reading of the signs of our time should help us discover a grammar of synodality for our time. In grammar there are some basic rules which never change. For us, these are the rules of Catholicity, such as the dignity stemming from Baptism; the role of Peter in the church; episcopal collegiality; ordained ministry, the common priesthood of the faithful and their interrelation (cf. *LG*, no. 10). With these fundamental elements of our Catholic grammar, we have to find the way to express the new insights the Holy Spirit gives us.⁶

He then explained the division of the work and the procedures of the assembly.

## WORKING GROUPS ON SYNOD METHODOLOGY: THURSDAY, OCTOBER 5

On Thursday, October 5, the working groups (*circuli minores*) began meeting. Each engaged the "question for discernment" entrusted to it. Each group summarized the results of the discernment in a written report of two pages. The report collected points of convergence and divergence, tensions that have emerged, and questions that remain open. It also contained insights and proposals for concrete steps to be taken in relation to the issues addressed.

At the end of the first two sessions, each working group identified the most significant points in the report it wanted to share and, above all, the questions and proposals to submit to the assembly by way of a concise three-minute intervention, that will be read in the following General Congregation. The report and the intervention outlined the consensus reached and made explicit any divergences. The report had to be approved by an absolute majority of the members who attest that it faithfully represents the work of the group.

Each working group included an expert-facilitator, who accompanied the exchanges from a methodological point of view and ensured the flow of the process. Each group also had an appointed secretary, but elected a rapporteur at the beginning of the proceedings. They oversaw the draft and final text of the report. The rapporteur also read the brief intervention on behalf of the group in General Congregation and delivered the final text of the report to the General Secretariat.

The General Congregations received and listened to the contributions of the working groups. By way of the free interventions made in Plenary Assembly, they contributed to discernment through the discussion of what emerged from the working groups. In this way, they enabled the working

---

6. Synod of Bishops, "XVI General Ordinary Assembly." Unless otherwise noted, all quotes in the following pages are from this list of resources.

groups to reread and modify their conclusions in light of the many other perspectives that emerged during the plenary debate.[7]

## FOURTH GENERAL CONGREGATION: MONDAY, OCTOBER 9

### Presentation by Cardinal Hollerich

The General Relator, Jean-Claude Cardinal Hollerich, introduced module 1, "Communion."

> In brief, our work will be divided into five modules. The first four will be devoted to discernment on the issues proposed in the *Instrumentum laboris*, following the order of its parts (Sections A, B1, B2, B3) and using the Worksheets prepared for this purpose. The work in the *circuli minores* will follow the method of conversation in the Spirit. Experts will have the certainly demanding task of progressively synthesizing the fruits of the work of the *circuli minores* and the General Congregations in view of the drafting of the Synthesis Report. It [Conversation in the Spirit] aims to build consensus without dividing into factions or crushing into uniformity. In this way it fosters the passage from listening to one another to listening to the Spirit. At the end of each module, after the work in groups and the discussion in plenary, each of the *circuli minores* will be called upon to draw up a Report of the work done, expressing what there is agreement on, but also any differences or questions on which to continue reflection. Ideally this road map should indicate where we feel consensus has been reached among us and above all within the People of God, laying down possible steps to undertake as a response to the voice of the Spirit. But it should also say where deeper reflection is needed and what could help that process of reflection.

At appropriate points, Fr. Timothy Radcliffe OP, Professor Anna Rowlands, and a number of Sisters gave spiritual and theological inputs respectively on the matters under discussion.

---

7. It should be noted that this differs from the usual practice in synods until now. As remarked above, until this synod, the normal thing had been to begin with plenary assemblies in which each bishop who wished could speak for eight minutes. The Relator summarized the discussion in a long speech. Then followed the *circuli minores* in language groupings to develop proposals for voting.

## Testimonies

Four testimonies were heard. Sônia Gomes de Oliveira gave testimony about ministry with migrants and prostitutes in Brazil.

His Eminence, Metropolitan of Pisidia, Job (Getcha) set forth the meaning and practice of "synod" in the Orthodox Communion.

> For the Orthodox, synodality corresponds to the practice established by the first ecumenical council (Nicea, 325) of gathering the bishops of a region at least twice a year under the presidency of their *prōtos* (cf. canon 5). This synodality is best described by Apostolic Canon 34. . . . A synod is a **deliberative** meeting of **bishops**, not a consultative clergy-laity assembly. . . . However, in certain historical circumstances, the Orthodox Church has involved the clergy and laity in synodal decision-making. For example, in the Ottoman empire, the election of Primates was carried out by clergy-laity assemblies. . . . In the Church of Cyprus, until today, bishops are elected not exclusively by the episcopate, but also by the clergy and the laity: at the first stage, the entire population of the Island votes from the list of all the candidates, then, in a second step, the synod of bishops chooses one from the three candidates having obtained the majority of votes.

The third testimony was given by P. Clarence Davedassan (Malaysia). "Except for the Philippines and Timor Leste, Christianity remains a small minority in most parts of Asia," comprising only 3.31 percent of the population of the four billion people in Asia. Yet, "in many parts of Asia, the church takes the lead in the service of integral human development and the common good, especially in the fields of education, healthcare, and reaching out to the poor and marginalised groups in society beyond the boundaries of our churches." The Basic Ecclesial Communities "(in some places known as Small Christian Communities or Basic Human Communities) bring about not only spiritual transformation but also social transformation."

The final testimony for the day came from Siu Wai Vanessa Cheng.

> The Church in Asia chose the image of "Taking Off Our Shoes" to describe the Asian synodal journey. It is a beautiful sign of respect and also an expression of Asians' deep awareness of the holy. . . . Many Asian cultures do not favor outspokenness for a variety of reasons, such as the fear of making mistakes and losing "face" . . . As a result, many faithful may tend to remain silent instead of

voicing their own views and concerns. Therefore, we need to pay even more attention to those who are silent for some reason.

## SIXTH GENERAL CONGREGATION: FRIDAY, OCTOBER 13

Introducing the day's work, "Co-responsibility in Mission" (module 3, section B2 of the *Instrumentum laboris*), the General Relator, Cardinal Hollerich, spoke of the "digital continent": "Many of us see the internet as simply a tool for evangelisation. It is more than that. It transforms our ways of living, of perceiving reality, and of living relations. Thus, it becomes a new mission territory. Just as Francis Xavier left for new lands, are we willing and prepared to sail towards this new continent?"

He observed that, "Most of us are men. But men and women receive the same baptism and the same Spirit. The baptism of women is not inferior to the baptism of men. How can we ensure that women feel they are an integral part of this missionary church?"

The spiritual reflection from Mother Maria Ignazia Angelini, OSB, asked the delegates to "imagine a process of struggling to understand." She insisted that "difference—even to the point of conflict—however necessary and fruitful in the church, nevertheless differs from quarrelsome and poisoned contention, because it never demonizes the opponent, but makes room for him or her."

Fr. Carlos Maria Galli in his theological input, stated "not only that the church has a mission, but that the mission of the Triune God has a church. Synodality is missionary, mission is synodal. The movement goes from 'us' to 'I': the church is the communal subject of the mission, and within her, each person is called to evangelize."

## Testimonies

In the first testimony, Sr. Gloria Liliana Franco Echeverri, ODN, told of Doña Rosa, seventy years old, who visits the sick in her neighborhood every evening, ensuring they have food and a dignified life. Until six months ago, she also brought them communion. However, the new priest told her that this task was no longer for her. Now, male Eucharistic ministers, equipped with striking uniforms, will deliver communion. She also spoke of Martha, who completed her doctorate in theology with better grades than her male counterparts. The Pontifical University she graduated from decided not to give her a canonical degree because she's a woman. Instead, she received a civil title. Yet this is progress, as until recently women in her country couldn't study theology, only religious sciences!

Sister Xiskya Lucia Valladares Paguaga, RP, and Mr. José Manuel De Urquidi Gonzalez shared their experience of the Digital Synod, a project called "The Church Listens to You." Begun with 250 digital evangelists (63 percent laypeople, 27 percent priests, and 10 percent religious brothers and sisters), it conducted listening sessions in 115 countries, in seven languages, and reaching a total of 150,000 people who answered the questionnaire, 30 percent of whom were non-believers and people distant from the church. Eventually, a network of these evangelists was created, amounting to about two thousand digital evangelists. Some of these missionaries (577 from 68 countries) met in person for the first time for the Mass and Blessing of Digital Evangelizers and Missionaries during the Youth Day in Lisbon (August 2023).

They target persons between eighteen and forty years old.

> These are those who believe "without belonging," the distanced and alienated, the "Nones" as they are called in English. They are those who left the church, hurt by so much discrimination, who got bored with our sermons, who did not understand our language or perhaps never set foot in a church. But they continue searching. They spend a large part of their hours online because they are "partially hidden" there. Their anonymity allows them to overcome shame and distance, or just to ask questions. Engaging in dialogue with them requires time, patience, and much love.

Finally, Cardinal Stephen Ameyu Martin Mulla, Archbishop of Juba (South Sudan) spoke on the bishop's ministry from a missionary synodal perspective. The bishop should encourage the mutual collaboration of all in evangelizing witness based on everyone's gifts and roles, without clericalizing lay people and without turning the clergy into lay people.

## GERMAN SYNODAL WAY: PRESS CONFERENCE

On October 14, Bishop Georg Bätzing of Limburg, writing in his role as co-president of the German Synodal Way, shared with the synod participants a 159-page document translated into various languages, providing the decisions taken by the German Synodal Way. Among them are votes calling for reevaluating homosexuality, blessing homosexual unions, and ending mandatory priest celibacy. It also addresses gender diversity, women in sacramental ministries, and involving laypeople in selecting diocesan bishops. The German Synodal Process Statutes provide for these to be sent as propositions to the Holy Father.[8]

At a Synod Press Briefing on Saturday, October 21, Bishop Franz Josef Overbeck of Essen acknowledged people's concerns about the German Synodal Way. He referred to Germany's particular cultural situation to justify some of the proposals. In his thirteen years as bishop of Essen, he ordained only fifteen new priests, while three hundred priests died. Currently the diocese has no seminarians in formation. This is one reason to explore an end to mandatory priestly celibacy. He previously said that the synod on synodality must take up the proposals advanced by the German Synodal Way, "from the role of women to the question of sexuality and the question of people who love each other." However, he noted that the synod's "Conversation in the Spirit method," emphasizing listening without asking questions and creating times of silent prayer, could be incorporated into the German Synodal Way's work going forward.[9]

## TWELFTH GENERAL CONGREGATION: WEDNESDAY, OCTOBER 18

Cardinal Jean-Claude Hollerich introduced module B3: "Participation, Governance and Authority." He explained the paths ahead.

> The results of this first session will have to be disseminated, involving our bishops' conferences, reconvening the synodal teams, activating the appropriate forms of communication, preparing the paths of experimentation and in-depth study that we will identify together as appropriate. [Also,] we will immediately have to start planning how to collect the feedback from the local churches, the fruits of the exchanges and the experimentation and deepening paths, so as to arrive "prepared" for the second session, [having] a clearer awareness by the People of God as to what it means to be a synodal church, and above all what steps the Lord is asking us to take to become one and thus better proclaim his Gospel.

---

8. Gagliarducci, "Synod on Synodality 2023."
9. Liedl, "German Bishop at Synod on Synodality."

Fr. Timothy Radcliffe, OP gave a spiritual reflection. His "American brethren gave [him] a T-shirt which said, 'Have a good crisis!'"

> Often people have told [him], "This synod will not change anything." Some with hope and some with fear. That is a lack of faith in the name of the Lord, "the name which is above every name" (Phil 2.9).... A man was lost in Ireland. He asked a farmer, "How do I get to Dublin?" The farmer replied, "If I wanted to go to Dublin, I would not start here." But wherever people are, that is where the journey home starts, the home of the church and the home of the kingdom.

The theological reflection by the Rev. Dario Vitali, coordinator of the expert theologians, explored what processes, structures, and institutions there might be in a missionary synodal church. *Lumen gentium*'s placing of chapter 2, the People of God, before chapter 3, the Hierarchy, was the "'Copernican revolution' of conciliar ecclesiology." It "breaks the ecclesiological pyramid built over the centuries: before functions comes the dignity of the baptized; before differences, which establish hierarchies, comes the equality of the children of God." Debates continued nevertheless.

> Emphasis on the ecclesiology of communion, primarily focused on hierarchical communion, has produced a true "centralization" of the church. On the other hand, some fear that synodality, understood as the "journeying together" of the People of God, constitutes an alternative to the principle of communion. In reality, synodality is none other than the very communion of the church as the Holy People of God. Synodality and communion can be identified with one another, as long as we understand the church as the People of God journeying together.... Without the synod, the practice of synodality would end up dissolving into a thousand streams, creating a quagmire, slowing down, if not preventing, the "walking together" of the People of God.

## Testimonies

Msgr. Shane Mackinlay, Bishop of Sandhurst, Australia, described what happened at the Fifth Plenary Council of Australia, held for over four years, from 2018 to 2022. The process began with a very broad consultation involving 220,000 people responding to the question, "What do you think God is asking of us in Australia at this time?" This led eventually to a set of eight papers being presented to the second assembly, which with various amendments made during the assembly became the eight decrees of the Council:

> reconciliation with indigenous people; healing the wounds caused by sexual abuse; missionary discipleship; witnessing to the equal dignity of women and men; spirituality and liturgy; formation for ministry; synodal models of governance, and integral ecology.

At least half of each day during the two assemblies was devoted to conversations in the spirit, beginning with extended prayer on a scriptural text, in table groups of about ten people, including a mix of bishops, priests, religious, and lay people. "There were 280 members, with about 60 percent specified by canon law and the remaining members being proposed from parishes, dioceses and other groups in the church." There was widespread distress when voting on the initial version of the decree relating to the equal dignity of women and men failed to achieve the required two-thirds majority among the bishops.

> We decided to suspend the planned agenda, to give space for concerns from all perspectives and all members to be articulated, initially through Conversation in the Spirit in our table groups, but then also in the whole assembly. Eventually we established a special drafting group, and returned to the topic two days later, where a revised text was passed overwhelmingly. In hindsight I believe what happened was that people spoke much more from the heart, with a vulnerability that exposed them personally, putting themselves on the line to describe their lived experience of how they were personally affected. Beyond the content of the decrees, I think the most significant impact of the Plenary Council on the Church in Australia will be the positive and transformative experience of discernment and synodality, which is now clearly established as the normal way for approaching discussions and shared decision-making in all our activities.

Msgr. Alexandre Joly, Bishop of Troyes, spoke on the role of the bishop. When he consulted the priests, deacons, and various lay leaders in the diocese for a new vicar general, some of the responses were that a deacon or a lay person should be the vicar general, which is not allowed under canon law. So, he put another person he called a delegate general alongside the vicar general.

> A faithful laywoman had recently become available and was recognised by all for her commitment and competence in the service of the diocese. She is now part of the executive trio, working in concert with the vicar general, and in deep communion with me. She now acts as the Curia's moderator for the diocese's pastoral services and oversees the diocese's pastoral and missionary transformation.

Estela P. Padilla, FABC-OTC presented "'Take Off Your Shoes': The Asian Journey into Synodal Leadership." She was the sole lay woman member of the team.

> In one of the synodal consultations, an Indian bishop said, "I have a problem with the Holy Spirit. I doubt if the Holy Spirit can really lead the church. We were full of Spirit after Vatican II," yet sixty years later the church is on its lowest credibility standing due to sexual and other forms of abuse, etc. One priest asked me why our report is so full of negative things happening in the church. Where is the good news there? I told him, the good news is the honesty in facing all the woundedness of our world and our failure of bearing witness to the Good News in the midst of poverty, violence brought by terrorism, and political oppression, adding to the pain of clericalism and hierarchical leadership. I actually found these negative comments on the church liberating, because as Asians we don't like conflicts; we always seek harmony. Harmony is of course positive except when it hinders us from naming what is wrong.

## SIXTEENTH GENERAL CONGREGATION: MONDAY, OCTOBER 23

Cardinal Charles BO, SDB, Archbishop of Yangon and Myanmar and President of the Federation of Asian Bishops Conferences (FABC), preached the homily at the mass in St. Peter's. "The documents [of Pope Francis] call for a threefold reconciliation to save humanity and the planet: reconciliation with God (*Evangelii gaudium*), reconciliation with nature (*Laudato Si*), and reconciliation with one another (*Fratelli tutti*). Our synodal journey is about healing and reconciling the world in justice and peace."

In his spiritual reflection, Fr. Timothy Radcliffe, OP, characterized the moment as one of waiting. He repeated the words of Simone Weil he quoted during the retreat. "We do not obtain the most precious gifts by going in search of them but by waiting for them. This way of looking is, in the first place, attentive. The soul empties itself of all its own contents in order to receive the human being it is looking at, just as he or she is, in all their truth."[10]

Sr. Maria Grazia Angelini, OSB, commented on the parable of the mustard seed. It is a matter of seizing—among the many words heard—"the smallest," full of the future, and daring to imagine how to deliver it to the earth that will make it mature and become a hospitable place.

Fr. Ormond Rush[11] tried to ease the inner struggle of some over tradition and truth. A similar dis-ease appeared during Vatican II. Citing Ratzinger,[12] he underlined two understandings of tradition: a "static" understanding and a "dynamic" understanding. The former is legalistic, propositional, and ahistorical (i.e., relevant for all times and places); the latter is personalist, sacramental, and rooted in history, and therefore to be interpreted with an historical consciousness. The Council used the phrase "living tradition" to describe the latter (*DV*, 12). It says, "There is a growth in insight into the realities and words that are being passed on" (*DV*, 8). This divine revelation is presented as an ongoing encounter in the present, and not just something that happened in the past. Vatican II, accordingly, urged the church to be ever attentive to the movements of the revealing and saving God present and active in the flow of history, by attending to "the signs of the times" in the light of the living Gospel (*GS*, 4).

## EIGHTEENTH GENERAL CONGREGATION: WEDNESDAY, OCTOBER 25

Pope Francis addressed the assembly. He explained the infallibility in belief (*in credendo falli nequit*, LG 9) of the People of God thus: "when you want to know what Holy Mother Church believes, go to the magisterium because its task is to teach it to you. But when you want to know how the church believes, go to the faithful people." He recalled how, at the Council of Ephesus (431) the people lined both sides of the street leading to the cathedral while the bishops were processing toward the entrance, and they were repeating in chorus: "Mother of God," asking the hierarchy to declare as dogma this truth that they possessed as the People of God. "When the ministers exceed their service and mistreat the People of God, they disfigure the face

---

10. Weil, *Waiting on God*, 169.
11. Author of the impressive book *Vision of Vatican II*.
12. See throughout Ratzinger, "Transmission of Divine Revelation," 181–98.

of the church with machismo and dictatorial attitudes (it is enough to recall the intervention of Sr. Liliana Franco). It is painful to find in some parish offices the 'price list' for sacramental services, similar to a supermarket." "Clericalism is a thorn, it is a scourge, it is a form of worldliness that defiles and damages the face of the Lord's bride; it enslaves the holy, faithful People of God."

An initial Draft Summary was presented to the assembly in the morning and voted paragraph by paragraph, each paragraph needing the approval of two-thirds of members present. Amendments could call for elimination, addition, or replacement of passages.[13] Eventually 1,025 amendments were received from the assembly, then 126 additional amendments from individuals.

The *Letter of the XVI General Assembly of the Synod of Bishops to the People of God* was published on this day. The voting on this was 336/12.

## *CIRCULI MINORES*: THURSDAY, OCTOBER 26

The amendments to the Draft Summary were deliberated in the small groups (*circuli minores*).[14]

## TWENTIETH GENERAL CONGREGATION: SATURDAY, OCTOBER 28

Following a break on October 27, the amended text was presented in the synod hall as the *Synthesis Report*; it was voted on and approved by the members of the synod.

The assembly concluded with *Te Deum* ("To You, O God"), a traditional song of praise and thanksgiving at the end of solemnities in the church, after a victory in war, or coronation of a king, or salvation from some difficult experience.

---

13. Liedl, "Synod on Synodality."
14. On October 26, Bishop Athanasius Schneider held a book event steps from St. Peter's Square. He was launching his book *Credo: Compendium of the Catholic Faith*, published in September. He castigated Pope Francis' recent restrictions on the celebration of the 1962 Order of Mass. For him, Francis' two volumes on the environment (*Laudato Si' and Laudate Deum*) were "ecological mysticism" and "idolatry." He criticized gender ideology and chastised bishops who closed their churches during the COVID-19 pandemic. See Giangravé, "Papal Critic Praises Dubia."

Cardinal Mario Grech, OSA, General Secretary of the Synod of Bishops

# 11

# Synod Letter to the People of God and Context of the *Synthesis Report*

## SYNOD LETTER TO THE PEOPLE OF GOD

THE ASSEMBLY SPOKE OF a "beautiful and enriching experience."[1] They noted how unprecedented the experience was: "For the first time, at Pope Francis' invitation, men and women have been invited, in virtue of their baptism, to sit at the same table to take part, not only in the discussions, but also in the voting process of this assembly of the Synod of Bishops." They listened to the Word of God and each other's experience, "together, in the complementarity of our vocations, our charisms and our ministries." We hope that the months leading to the second session in October 2024 will allow everyone to concretely participate in the dynamism of missionary communion indicated by the word "synod."

> It is "trust" that gives us the audacity and inner freedom that we experienced, not hesitating to freely and humbly express our convergences, differences, desires and questions. There are multiple challenges and numerous questions: the *Synthesis Report* of the first session will specify the points of agreement we have reached,

---

1. All quotes in this section are from Synod of Bishops, "Letter of the XVI Ordinary General Assembly."

highlight the open questions, and indicate how our work will proceed.

Above all, the church of our time has the duty to listen, in a spirit of conversion, to those who have been victims of abuse committed by members of the ecclesial body . . . to families, to their educational concerns, to the Christian witness they offer in today's world . . . the voice of those who want to be involved in lay ministries and to participate in discernment and decision-making structures.

To progress further in synodal discernment, the church particularly needs to gather even more the words and experience of the ordained ministers: priests, the primary collaborators of the bishops, whose sacramental ministry is indispensable for the life of the whole body; deacons, who, through their ministry, signify the care of the entire church for the most vulnerable. She needs to let herself be questioned by the prophetic voice of consecrated life, the watchful sentinel of the Spirit's call. She also needs to be attentive to all those who do not share her faith but are seeking the truth, and in whom the Spirit, who "offers everyone the possibility of being associated with this paschal mystery" (*GS*, no. 22), is also present and operative.

## WHAT CHANGED BETWEEN THE DRAFT SUMMARY AND THE *SYNTHESIS REPORT*?

I did not find the Draft Summary on the Synod Secretariat web site. Journalists at hand apparently received copies. I rely here on two of them.[2]

One of the most notable differences between the two texts is the disappearance of the references to "divorced people in second unions" and "people who identify as LGBTQ+." These words have been replaced by a more general proposal referring to "people who feel marginalized or excluded [. . .] because of their marital status, identity or/and sexuality" (16, h). The *Synthesis Report*, however, did once use the term "sexual identity" (14, g).

The text has been extensively reworked; it is more incisive on the need to consider the role of women. As a result, women appear more as protagonists and are included more than in the first version, which referred to their "needs," a word that has been removed. In the new text, it is the assembly—and not just the women on their own—that calls for "a church in which

---

2. Liedl, "Synod on Synodality"; Aleteia, "Synod: How over 1200 Amendments."

men and women dialogue together" so as to be "together as protagonists, without subordination, exclusion, and competition" (9, h).[3]

In terms of novelties, the *Report* denounces the condition of consecrated women "too often considered as cheap labor." There is also a call for women judges in all canonical trials, and for "the feminine contribution" to be valued in the training of priests.[4]

Language suggesting the need to reconsider the extent to which "sexual difference should shape ecclesiology and approaches to ministry," an apparent reference to the church's understanding that only men are eligible to be ordained to holy orders, and therefore exercise certain ministries of teaching, governance, and sanctification, was also removed.

An addition was a proposal to place men who have left the priesthood into "a pastoral service that enhances their training and experience" on a case-by-case basis (13, k).

A proposal that a group of experts engage in "shared discernment" on controversial "doctrinal, pastoral and ethical issues," including issues related to gender, sexuality, and the end of life, was tweaked to underscore that this discernment should be conducted "in light of the Word of God, church teaching, theological reflections, and, valuing the synod experience" (15, k).[5] However, the final document added the possibility of listening to "people directly affected by the matters under consideration." Here the church shows the will to better listen to people living in situations she deems irregular.[6]

Absent from the final text was a proposal in the draft "to establish a permanent synod of bishops elected by episcopal conferences to support the Petrine ministry." Instead, in its place was language that had not been in the draft version about making the Council of Cardinals, a group of nine senior prelates who advise the pope, a "synodal council." "This phrase is ambiguous; given the association between synodality and greater involvement of non-bishops, it's not unreasonable to think it's pointing to the participation of non-Cardinals in the 'Pope's cabinet' in some way—perhaps even religious sisters and laywomen."[7]

---

3. Aleteia, "Synod: How over 1200 Amendments."
4. Aleteia, "Synod: How over 1200 Amendments."
5. Liedl, "Synod on Synodality."
6. Aleteia, "Synod: How over 1200 Amendments."
7. Liedl, "Synod on Synodality."

Synodality represents "the future of the church" (1, e). An earlier version contained the assertion that "any step backwards seems impossible," which smacks of language of the German Synodal Way.[8]

Certain usages of the word "ministry" have been changed to improve its etymology and point to "service." A new paragraph asks for "any ambiguities" to be clarified regarding the term "an all-ministerial church" (8, m) used in the *Instrumentum laboris*.

In the section on bishops, the request to verify the criteria for selecting candidates for the episcopate is now qualified with "balancing the authority of the Apostolic Nuncio with participation of episcopal conferences" (12, l).

The *Report* included a proposal found nowhere in the draft to carefully examine "whether it is appropriate to ordain prelates of the Roman Curia as bishops" (13, k), "possibly the latest instance of decoupling episcopal ordination from church governance," a concern during the Francis pontificate.[9]

Many amendments seem to represent the perspective of the South. To the categories of marginalized people, the text adds "Afro-descendant peoples" and victims of racism. The text now added the phrase "even genocide" in the sentence "in some places, the proclamation of the Gospel was associated with colonization, *even genocide*" (5, e). Naming countries at war as Ukraine, the Holy Land, and the Middle East has been removed, leaving only the generic phrase "many countries on several continents." "This suggests a protest from African countries in particular, which are prey to many forgotten conflicts."[10]

## THE OUTLINE OF THE *SYNTHESIS REPORT*

On October 28, the amended text of the Summary, now called the *Synthesis Report*, was presented and the 372 proposals were overwhelmingly approved.

The subtitle, "A Synodal Church in Mission," highlights the interpenetration of synod and mission, also manifested in the title of Part II, "All Disciples, all Missionaries." A synodal church is a church internally organized and journeying together on mission for the kingdom. There is an Introduction and Conclusion ("Proceeding along the Journey"). The body consists of three parts:

8. Aleteia, "Synod: How over 1200 Amendments."
9. Liedl, "Synod on Synodality."
10. Aleteia, "Synod: How over 1200 Amendments."

## Understanding the Synod on Synodality, 2023 Session

Part I: The Face of the Synodal Church

Part II: All Disciples, all Missionaries

Part III: Weaving Bonds, Building Communities.

Each of the twenty chapters is organized in three sections: convergences, matters for consideration, and proposals. A quick word count establishes the following dominant words/concepts:

- Synodality, 61 times;
- Bishop, 61 times (includes Bishop of Rome, College of Bishops, but not Synod of Bishops)
- Episcopal, 39 (conferences, 20; ministry, 9; college, 5; assembly, authority, bodies, life, 1 each)
- Priests, 24 times (excluding common priesthood, priesthood of Christ)
- Charisms, 22 times (charisms and ministries, 9; charismatic, 7)
- Accompaniment, 16 times (accompanying, 7; accompany, 7)
- Co-responsibility, 15 times (co-responsible, 3)
- Eucharist, 15 times (eucharistic, 1; baptism, 12; baptismal, 3)
- Holy Spirit, 12 times (conversation in the Spirit, 7);
- Trinity/Trinitarian, 6 times

The episcopal ministry is still dominant, though now to be exercised through affective and effective synodality. The concepts of charisms, co-responsibility, and accompaniment indicate the synodal manner of pastoral care.

## HERMENEUTICS OF THE TEXT

Texts have a surplus of meaning, deriving from many factors. As regards Vatican II texts, Rush posited that they were sometimes

> deliberately expressed either in an open-ended way or with juxtapositions of traditional and innovative formulations. Interpretation of such passages requires particular attention to *interrelating a hermeneutics of the text with a hermeneutics of the authors* . . . the juxtaposition in the final texts is not so much one of contradictory

views but rather of differing perspectives on the same mystery. A "trajectory" toward a newer understanding of an issue is often evident, and this trajectory must be given a certain weight in the interpretation of the text.[11]

The drafters of the *Synthesis Report* had just one day to edit 1,151 amendments. The goal was arriving at quick consensus in the assembly. One is not surprised by the juxtaposition of apparently contrasting positions, statements that qualify or redirect what went before, but the trajectory of the texts is, nevertheless, clear.

Normally the synod required a two-thirds majority for proposals to carry. In this one, the consensus-seeking method and perhaps the clear delineation of convergences, matters for consideration, and proposals produced an outstanding result. Outside the two proposals on ministry for women, which carried by 80 percent, the rest mostly carried by 95 percent and over. This means that despise the noise of some, the church all over the world is well united on the journey.

The *Synthesis Report* had twenty chapters, each chapter arranged in letter paragraphs. In citations here, the numeral refers to the chapter, the letter to the paragraph. For example, "16, h," means chapter 16, paragraph h. The figures after this represent the voting: 340/4 means 340 ayes, 4 noes.

Since the *Report* covers ground already in some measure traversed by the *IL* and *DCS*, I choose to highlight only some of the 372 propositions, especially those that call for commentary. I often cite relevant parts of the text verbatim, to allow the text to speak for itself and dialogue with the ensuing commentary. I have not followed the organization and order of the twenty chapters; rather my organization and chapter headings are part of my interpretation of the text. I gather together aspects of a topic scattered in different chapters of the *Report*. The flow represents an "inverse pyramid"—matters pertaining to Christ's faithful are at the top. The text of the *Report* is indented.

---

11. Rush, *Vision of Vatican II*, 4, 5 (italics original).

# 12

# The *Synthesis Report* with Commentary

## SYNODALITY

Synodality translates the Trinitarian dynamism with which God comes to meet humanity into spiritual attitudes and ecclesial processes (2, a; 340/4).

Its orientation is towards mission, and its practice involves gathering in assembly at each level of ecclesial life. It involves reciprocal listening, dialogue, community discernment, and creation of consensus as an expression that renders Christ present in the Holy Spirit, each taking decisions in accordance with their responsibilities (1, h; 340/4).

Synodality grows when each member is involved in processes and decision-making for the mission of the church (18, e; 340/6).

The assembly proposes to promote theological deepening of the terminological and conceptual understanding of the notion and practice of synodality before the second session of the assembly, drawing on the rich heritage of theological research since the Second Vatican Council and in particular the documents of the International Theological Commission on *Synodality in the Life and Mission of the Church* (2018) and *Sensus fidei in the Life of the Church* (2014) (1, p; 339/5).

## Commentary

THE SYNOD EVOKED VARIOUS aspects of synodality: journeying together and listening to each other; intrinsically oriented toward mission; grows when each member is involved in decision-making. There is agreement that "with the necessary clarifications synodality represents the future of the church" (1, q). That the assembly acknowledged the work of the ITC (*Synodality in the Life and Mission of the Church* and *Sensus Fidei in the Life of the Church*), yet called for theological deepening of the concept of synodality, indicates puzzle about the possible ramifications. Hence the call to clarify the canonical implications of synodality. Nevertheless, the call for revising the Code of Canon Law accordingly shows the desire for synodality to transition from "spiritual attitudes" to concrete "ecclesial processes."

Halík hopes that other churches, ecclesial communities, and other religions could be included in the synodal process: "a process of listening to each other and finding a way forward together . . . would be an important step toward that universal fraternity of which Pope Francis writes in his encyclical *Fratelli tutti*."[1]

## BAPTISM, FOUNDATION AND SOURCE OF MISSION AND PARTICIPATION

> Before any distinction of charisms and ministries, "we were all baptized by one Spirit into one body" (1 Cor 12:13). Therefore, among all the baptized, there is a genuine equality of dignity and a common responsibility for mission, according to the vocation of each. By the anointing of the Spirit, who "teaches all things" (1 John 2:27), all believers possess an instinct for the truth of the Gospel, the *sensus fidei*. This consists in a certain connaturality with divine realities and the aptitude to grasp what conforms to the truth of faith intuitively" (3, c; 318/26).
>
> We need more creativity in establishing ministries according to the needs of local churches, with the particular involvement of the young. One can think of further expanding responsibilities assigned to the existing ministry of lector[2]. . . This could become a fuller ministry of the Word of God, which, in appropriate contexts, could also include preaching. We could also explore the possibility

---

1. Halík, *Afternoon of Christianity*, 209.
2. Pope Francis opened this up to women in January 2021.

of establishing a ministry assigned to married couples committed to supporting family life and accompanying people preparing for the Sacrament of Marriage (8, n; 308/38).

From the Eucharist we learn to articulate unity and diversity: unity of the church and multiplicity of Christian communities; unity of the sacramental mystery and variety of liturgical traditions; unity of celebration and diversity of vocations, charisms, and ministries. Nothing shows more than the Eucharist that the harmony created by the Spirit is not uniformity[3] and that every ecclesial gift is intended for common edification (3, f; 340/4).

The assembly asks that we avoid repeating the mistake of talking about women as an issue or a problem. Instead, we desire to promote a church in which men and women dialogue together, in order to understand more deeply the horizon of God's project, that sees them together as protagonists, without subordination, exclusion and competition (9, h; 336/10).

Different positions have been expressed regarding women's access to the diaconal ministry. For some, this step would be unacceptable because they consider it a discontinuity with Tradition. For others, however, opening access for women to the diaconate would restore the practice of the early church. Others still, discern it as an appropriate and necessary response to the signs of the times, faithful to the Tradition . . . Some express concern that the request speaks of a worrying anthropological confusion, which, if granted, would marry the church to the spirit of the age (9, j; 277/69).

Women's access to formation programs and theological study needs to be considerably expanded. Women should also be integrated into seminary teaching and training programs to foster better formation for ordained ministry (9, p; 330/6).

We propose that women receive appropriate formation to enable them to be judges in all canonical processes (9, r; 323/23).

We believe the time has come for a revision of the 1978 document *Mutuae relationes*, regarding the relationships between bishops and religious in the church. We propose that this revision be completed in a synodal manner, consulting all involved (10, g; 338/8).

---

3. "The harmony created by the Spirit is not uniformity" paraphrases part of Pope Francis' "Opening of the Works" (see above).

## Commentary

Equal dignity in Baptism mandates co-responsibility in mission, according to the charism and vocation of each. The synod also called for the clarification of the term "ministry."[4] The reader should consult the question of jurisdiction below (under "Bishops"), also the "Debate about the Origin of Power of Governance in the Church" (see above). A theologian, John Cavadini, insists that governance in the church derives from the Eucharist, not baptism.[5]

Elsewhere, the synod qualified the *sensus fidei*: "A mature exercise of the *sensus fidei* requires not only reception of Baptism but a life lived in authentic discipleship that develops the grace of Baptism. This enables us to distinguish the action of the Spirit from merely dominant forms of thinking or cultural conditioning, or from matters inconsistent with the Gospel. Understanding the exercise of the *sensus fidei* is to be deepened with appropriate theological reflection" (3, h; 337/7).[6]

This synod is insistent on the role of women in the church. The assembly, not just women on their own, calls for "a church in which men and women dialogue together" so as to be "together as protagonists, without subordination, exclusion, and competition." Two commissions appointed by Pope Francis studied the matter of diaconate for women without conclusion. The assembly called for renewed theological and pastoral research

---

4. On ministries for laity, it is interesting that the dioceses of Essen and Rottenburg-Stuttgart in Germany have commissioned twenty-six non-ordained theologians, men and women, to administer the sacrament of baptism in church liturgies. KNA International, "Male and Female Lay Theologians."

5. Cavadini, "Need for a Deeper Theology." For him, "an adequate theology of co-responsibility cannot be articulated as merely a function of Baptism." He opines that "co-responsibility for mission here seems nearly indistinguishable from co-responsibility for governance, and 'synodality' seems almost to mean 'co-responsibility for governance." A closer focus on the church as mystery originating from Christ's sacrificial priesthood would show governance deriving from the Eucharist and pertaining to the fullness of Orders of the bishop. Baptism confers dignity and mission because it confers a share in Christ's priesthood on all the baptized. He echoes the 1917 Code of Canon Law and those who derive power of governance from ordination (see above).

6. This echoes the ITC, *Sensus fidei*, no. 57, which affirms that "since it is a property of the theological virtue of faith, the *sensus fidei fidelis* develops in proportion to the development of the virtue of faith ... and the *sensus fidei fidelis* is therefore proportional to the holiness of one's life." In no. 55 it affirms, "Although theological faith as such cannot err, the believer can still have erroneous opinions since all his thoughts do not spring from faith. Not all the ideas which circulate among the People of God are compatible with the faith" (CDF, *Donum Veritatis*, no. 35).

on the matter (9, n; 279/67). Furthermore, dioceses and institutes of consecrated life should follow the example of Pope Francis in promoting the participation of women in decision-making and in positions of responsibility in pastoral care and ministry. "Provisions need to be made in Canon Law accordingly" (9, m). The proposal of women as judges counters canon 1421 that states, "in each diocese the bishop is to appoint diocesan judges, who are to be clerics." It is interesting that a survey of Catholic women found that 78 percent support women preaching at mass, 68 percent back female ordination to the diaconate and priesthood, and a slim majority backs same-sex marriage in churches.[7]

A quick word search of *Mutuae relationes* in the *DCS* and in the *IL* turned up negative. The issue must have been first raised *in aula* itself, not surprising as misunderstandings, even conflicts, continue between diocesan bishops and religious institutes working in their dioceses.

The 1962 pre-Conciliar Missal is not mentioned in the *Synthesis Report*, nor was it in the *IL*. Yet, *DCS* (no. 92) reported that "the most common issue regarding the liturgy is the celebration of the pre-Conciliar Mass. The limited access to the 1962 Missal was lamented; many felt that the differences over how to celebrate the liturgy 'sometimes reached the level of animosity. People on each side of the issue reported feeling judged by those who differ from them'" (Ep. Conf. USA). It is possible that the assembly regarded the matter as closed by Pope Francis, motu proprio, *Traditionis custodes, On the Use of the Roman Liturgy Prior to the Reform of 1970*, July 16, 2021 (see above). I doubt we have seen the end of this discussion.

## BAPTISM, FOUNDATION OF ECUMENISM

> Baptism . . . also constitutes the foundation of ecumenism. Through it, all Christians participate in the *sensus fidei* and for this reason they should be listened to carefully, regardless of their tradition . . . There can be no synodality without an ecumenical dimension (7, b; 316/28).
>
> Another theme to be explored concerns the link between synodality and primacy at the various levels (local, regional, universal) in their mutual interdependence. We need a shared re-reading of

---

7. Lamb, "View from Rome," 31, reports this International Survey of Catholic Women, by the University of Newcastle, Australia, with 17,200 responses from 104 countries (two-thirds Western, English-speaking countries).

history in order to overcome stereotypes and prejudices. Ongoing ecumenical dialogues have provided a better understanding, in light of the practices of the first millennium, of the fact that synodality and primacy are related, complementary and inseparable realities. The clarification of this delicate point has consequences for the way of understanding the Petrine ministry in the service of unity, according to what St. John Paul II wished for in the encyclical *Ut unum sint* (7, h; 334/10).

The year 2025 marks the anniversary of the Council of Nicaea (325) at which the symbol of the faith that unites all Christians was elaborated. A common commemoration of this event will help us to better understand how in the past controversial questions were discussed and resolved together in Council (7, k; 340/1).

In the same year, 2025, providentially, the date of the solemnity of Easter will coincide for all churches and Christian communities. The assembly expressed a keen desire to come to a common date for the feast of Easter (7, l; 338/6).

A proposal has been put forward by some to convene an Ecumenical Synod on common mission in the contemporary world (7, n; 321/23).

## Commentary

That because of Baptism, other "Churches" and "Ecclesial Communities" participate in the *sensus fidei* is important. Agreement on the date of Easter would end the Quartodeciman Controversy already from the third and fourth centuries!

The invocation of Nicaea and its common creed challenges the church to advance on the path of ecumenism. The clarification of the connection between synodality and primacy, especially as it operated in the first thousand years, may be a windbreaker. An ecumenical synod on common mission in our world based on co-responsibility in mission for all the baptized would achieve a certain measure of unity, even if not yet at the Eucharistic level.

## ALL DISCIPLES, ALL MISSIONARIES

As members of the faithful People of God, all the baptized are co-responsible for mission . . . Therefore, all contribute to imagining and discerning steps to reform Christian communities and the church as a whole (18, a; 343/3).

Many of them [lay faithful] organize and animate pastoral communities, serve as religious educators, theologians and formators, spiritual animators and catechists, and participate in various parish and diocesan bodies. In many regions, the life of Christian communities and the mission of the church depend upon catechists. In addition, lay people serve in safeguarding and administration . . . for this reason, the acquisition of necessary competences should be provided for (8, e; 340/6)

The mission *ad gentes* is mutually enriching for the churches, because it not only involves the missionaries themselves but the entire community, which in this way is inspired to prayer, the sharing of goods, and witness. Churches lacking clergy should not give up this commitment, while those with more vocations to the ordained ministry benefit from cooperating pastorally in a genuinely evangelical manner. All the missionaries—laymen and women, those in consecrated life, deacons and priests, and particularly the members of missionary institutes and *fidei donum* missionaries—are an important resource for creating bonds of knowledge and exchange of gifts (8, g; 343/3).

Pastoral structures need to be re-organized so they can readily recognize, call forth, and animate lay charisms and ministries . . . Under the guidance of their pastors, the communities will be able to send people as well as sustain those they have sent on mission. In this way, these structures will primarily be at the service of the mission that the faithful carry out within society, in the family, and in work life, rather than focusing exclusively on internal matters or organizational concerns (8, l; 339/7).

If the mission is a grace involving all the church, the lay faithful contribute in a vital way to advancing that mission in all areas and in the ordinary situations of every day . . . in digital culture . . . in youth culture, in the world of work and business, politics, and the arts and culture; in scientific research, education, and training; in the care of our common home; and especially through participation in public life (8, d; 336/10).

Christians have a duty to commit themselves to active participation in building up the common good and defending the dignity of life, drawing inspiration from the church's social doctrine and working together in various ways, through engagement in civil society organizations, trade unions, popular movements, grassroots associations, in the field of politics, and so forth (4, g; 341/3).

The expression "an all-ministerial church," used in the *Instrumentum laboris*, can lend itself to misunderstanding. Its meaning will have to be clarified in order to remove any ambiguities (8, m; 331/15).[8]

We propose the establishment of a ministry of listening and accompaniment in order to give greater prominence to this service [of listening] (16, p; 327/19).

Based on the understanding of the People of God as the active subject of the mission of evangelization, we suggest legislating for the obligatory nature of Pastoral Councils in Christian communities and local churches (18, h; 321/25).

Could the canons referring to particular councils (plenary and provincial) be revised in order to increase the participation of the People of God, following the example of the dispensation obtained in the recent Plenary Council of Australia? (19, h; 330/16).

There are calls to make the Episcopal Council (canon 473 §4), the Diocesan Pastoral Council and the Eparchial Pastoral Council (CIC can. 511, CCEO can 272) mandatory, and to make the diocesan bodies exercising co-responsibility more operational, including in legal terms (12, k; 321/25).

## Commentary

"Rather than saying that the church has a mission, we affirm that church 'is' mission" (8, a).[9] Co-responsibility of all in mission must be the criterion underlying the structuring of Christian communities and the entire local

---

8. *IL*, B 2.2, d stated that "an all-ministerial church is not necessarily wholly a church of instituted ministries. Many ministries flow legitimately from the baptismal vocation, including spontaneous ministries and other recognized ministries that are not instituted and others that, by virtue of being instituted, receive a specific formation, mission, and stability."

9. This neatly summarizes *AG*, 2 (the pilgrim church is missionary by her very nature).

church with all its services, in all its institutions, in each of its pastoral bodies (cf. 1 Cor 12:4–31; 18, b; 333/13).

*Missio ad gentes* is redefined as mutual exchange of gifts among churches, in which even churches lacking clergy participate. The entire community sends out and supports its missionaries, be they laymen and women, those in consecrated life, deacons and priests, and particularly the members of missionary institutes and *fidei donum* missionaries. The mission perspectives here are particularly those of Paul VI, *Evangelii nuntiandi*, and Pope Francis, *Evangelii gaudium*.[10] In the "intensifying"[11] outlook of Vatican II, some take as their life's task what is common to all, as articulated in *AG*, 23.[12]

The assembly cautions that stress on lay mission in the world (4, g) "cannot become a pretext for assigning the care of the Christian community to bishops and priests alone" (18, b); however, without clericalizing the laity (8, f). The lay faithful already serve in different roles in the church (8, e; see above), in many regions, catechists preach and act as pastors of souls; necessary competencies are to be provided for these. Another number sees the "need to overcome the 'delegation' mindset found in so many areas of pastoral ministry" (14, f). Perhaps it needs be clarified what jurisdiction[13] a lay person in the church has by dint of baptism.[14] *IL* 2.2, a had forcefully called the church to overcome a vision that reserves any active function in the church to ordained ministers alone (bishops, priests, deacons), reducing the participation of the baptized to a subordinated collaboration.

In the Australian Plenary Council, bishops, clergy, religious, and laity, in all 280 persons, engaged in four years of consultation from 2018 to 2022. All had the vote and all signed the concluding statement.[15]

---

10. Ivereigh, *Wounded Shepherd*, 167, notes that *Evangelii gaudium* updates *Evangelii nuntiandi* in the light of the experience of Aparecida.

11. See Rush, *Vision of Vatican II*, 271. It is the attribution of a common task to a particular group in a more intensifying manner.

12. "[The Holy Spirit] inspires the missionary vocation in the hearts of individuals, and at the same time raises up in the church certain institutes which take as their own special task [*proprium officium*] the duty of preaching the Gospel, a duty belonging to the whole church."

13. The pastoral guidelines of the Congregation for Clergy, July 2020, forbade designating as "pastor" or "chaplain" laity or religious running parishes or similar works (no. 96), terms reserved for priests.

14. See Ligier, "'Lay Ministries,'" 175.

15. See the testimony of Msgr. Shane Mackinlay, Bishop of Sandhurst, Australia (Synod of Bishops, "XVI General Ordinary Assembly").

## FORMATION

> From the work of the assembly, there is a call for better knowledge of the teachings of Vatican II, post-conciliar teaching, and the church's social doctrine (5, o; 334/10).
>
> Formation for a synodal church needs to be undertaken synodally: the entire People of God being formed together as they journey together (14, f; 342/4).
>
> In the light of synodality, we propose that priority should be given to providing programs designed and intended for the joint formation of the entire People of God (laity, consecrated and ordained ministers) (14, k; 340/6).
>
> We recommend undertaking work on relationship and sexual education to accompany young people as they mature in their personal and sexual identities and to support the maturation of those called to celibacy and consecrated chastity. Formation in these areas is a necessary aid at all stages of life (14, g; 341/5).
>
> A thorough review of formation for ordained ministry in view of the missionary and synodal dimensions of the church is called for... (11, j; 331/15).
>
> In preparation for the next session of the assembly, a consultation of those responsible for the initial and ongoing formation of priests should be undertaken to assess how the synodal process is being received and to propose changes that will promote the exercise of authority in a style appropriate to a synodal church (14, o; 333/13).

## Commentary

Joint formation of the entire People of God, also in the teachings of Vatican II, post-conciliar teaching, and the church's social doctrine, will imprint the synodal outlook on the church. Though cost-intensive partly because it must respect the special situation of couples and families, it will demonstrate in practice the church's commitment to fostering synodality and the mission of all its baptized.

The call to accompany young people in relationship and sexual education and that human and sexual formation is necessary for "all stages of life" is fresh. This also concerns clergy, religious, and married couples! The church is moving from defense and prohibition in matters of sex to proactively offering formation.

## CHURCH ORDER

> The question of the relationship between the Sacrament of Holy Orders and jurisdiction needs to be studied in greater depth. In dialogue with *Lumen gentium* and more recent teachings such as the Apostolic Constitution *Praedicate evangelium*, the aim of such a study would be to clarify the theological and canonical criteria underlying the principle of the shared responsibility of the bishop and to determine the scope, forms, and implications of co-responsibility (12, g; 328/18).
>
> From the perspective of the uniqueness of ecclesial communion: how can we interweave the consultative and deliberative aspects of synodality? Given the variety of charismatic and ministerial gifts of the People of God, how do we integrate the tasks of advising, discerning, and deciding in the various participatory bodies (18, g; 336/10).
>
> The uncertainties surrounding the theology of the diaconate are related to the fact that it has only been restored to a distinct and permanent hierarchical ministry in the Latin Church since the Second Vatican Council (11, i; 286/61).
>
> As part of the rethinking of diaconal ministry, the church should promote a stronger orientation towards service to those who are poor (4, p; 337/7).
>
> Different opinions have been expressed about priestly celibacy. Some ask whether its appropriateness, theologically, for priestly ministry should necessarily translate into a disciplinary obligation in the Latin Church. This discussion is not new but requires further consideration (11, f; 291/55).
>
> The assembly calls for a review of the criteria for selecting candidates for the episcopate, balancing the authority of the Apostolic Nuncio with the participation of Episcopal Conferences. There are also requests to expand consultation with the faithful People of God, . . . and consecrated persons in the consultation process (12, l; 321/25).

It is proposed to enhance and strengthen the experience of the Council of Cardinals (C-9) as a synodal council at the service of the Petrine ministry (13, j; 319/27).

The doctrinal and juridical nature of episcopal conferences needs further study, recognizing the possibility of collegial action, including questions of doctrine that arise locally, thus reopening reflection on the Motu Proprio *Apostolos suos* (19, g; 312/34).

The presence of members other than bishops as witnesses to the synodal journey was appreciated. However, the question remains open about the effect of their presence as full members on the episcopal character of the assembly. Some see the risk that the specific task of the bishops will not be adequately understood. The criteria by which non-bishop members are called to be part of the Assembly will also need to be clarified (20, d; 327/19).

While at the regional level, it is possible to think of successive steps (an Ecclesial Assembly followed by an Episcopal Assembly), it is considered appropriate to clarify how this might be proposed with reference to the Catholic Church as a whole. Some believe that the formula adopted in this assembly responds to this need; others propose that an Episcopal Assembly follow an Ecclesial Assembly to conclude the discernment. Still, others prefer to reserve the role of members of the Synodal Assembly to the Bishops (20, f; 333/13).

## Commentary

*Praedicate evangelium*, in appointing lay faithful to positions hitherto reserved for clergy, sharpened the debate concerning *potestas regiminis* ("power of governance") in the church. The ITC, no. 69 seems to distinguish:

> between the process of *decision-making* through a joint exercise of discernment, consultation and co-operation, and *decision-taking*, which is within the competence of the bishop, the guarantor of apostolicity and catholicity. Working things out is a synodal task; decision is a ministerial responsibility.

However, ITC, no. 105 rightly classifies as an understanding of church not yet renewed by ecclesiology of communion, "the concentration of responsibility for mission in the ministry of pastors; insufficient appreciation of the consecrated life and charismatic gifts; rarely making use of the specific and qualified contribution of the lay faithful, including women, in their areas of expertise."

The question of the diaconate for women led to the call for ongoing reflection on the theology of the diaconate. Pope Benedict's *Omnium in mentem* made it clear that deacons do not act *in the person of* Christ. If the permanent diaconate is reimagined as more focused on the needs of the poor, the dispossessed, those that are marginalized, admitting women to the diaconate might prove feasible. It is to be noted, though, that many churches, especially in the South, never established the permanent diaconate in the first place.

The *Synthesis Report* passed over the question of priestly ordination for women, just as did *IL* (Worksheet B 2.34). *DCS*, no. 64 had noted that "much greater diversity of opinion was expressed on the subject of ordination for women, which some reports call for, while others consider a closed issue." In his response to the *Dubia* Cardinals, Pope Francis noted that Saint John Paul II's prohibition of priestly ordination for women as "definitive" did not make it a dogmatic definition, though to be adhered to by all. Even then, on June 1, 2021, Pope Francis had revised and reinforced canon 1379.

> *Canon 1379* (1983 Code)
>
> A person who, apart from the cases mentioned in can. 1378, pretends to administer a sacrament, is to be punished with a just penalty.

*Canon 1379* as revised June 2021, especially §3 is pertinent here:

> §1. The following incur a *latae sententiae*[16] interdict or, if a cleric, also a *latae sententiae* suspension:
>
> §3. Both a person who attempts to confer a sacred order on a woman, and the woman who attempts to receive the sacred order, incur a *latae sententiae* excommunication reserved to the Apostolic See; a cleric, moreover, may be punished by dismissal from the clerical state.
>
> §5. A person who, apart from the cases mentioned in §§1–4 and in can. 1384, pretends to administer a sacrament is to be punished with a just penalty.

The proposal about priestly celibacy (11, f) secured the second highest negative vote (291/55) after the question of women deacons. The bishops

---

16. *Latae sententiae* means "by the very fact itself, automatically."

of the October 2019 Amazon Synod[17] garnered more than the required two-thirds (128 votes to 41 against) for the proposition (Propositions 110 and 111) to ordain to the priesthood stably married men who have had a fruitful permanent diaconate and received adequate formation. The Papal Exhortation was still in writing when Benedict XVI and Cardinal Sarah issued a book[18] arguing that celibacy was intrinsic to the Catholic priesthood. Cardinal Sarah insisted that allowing a married clergy would be "a pastoral catastrophe" and would generate similar demands in other churches.

In January 2019, Pope Francis had said, "Personally, I think that celibacy is a gift to the church. I would say that I do not agree with allowing optional celibacy, no." He added at the time that he thought there was "room to consider some exceptions for married clergy" in the Latin Rite "when there is a pastoral necessity" in remote locations due to a lack of priests, such as in the Pacific Islands. In an interview on March 10, 2023, asked whether priestly celibacy "could be reviewed," the pope responded, "Yes, yes. In fact, everyone in the Eastern Church is married. Or those who want to. There they make a choice. Before ordination there is the choice to marry or to be celibate."[19]

The proposal of reinserting priests who left the ministry (11, l; 293/53) was not in the *IL*, which at B 2.4.9 had proposed ordaining the *viri probati*. However, *DCS*, 39 proposed, "Those who left ordained ministry and married, too, ask for a more welcoming church, with greater willingness to dialogue." Passed over is the proposal in *DCS*, no. 34 of appropriate forms of welcome and protection for the women and eventual children of priests who are at the risk of suffering serious injustice and discrimination.

The query whether it is appropriate to ordain Curia members bishops (13, k; 302/44) was not in the Summary, nor in the *IL* or *DCS*. Is it the latest instance of decoupling episcopal ordination from church governance, already encountered in *PE*?

The proposal of a Council of Cardinals (C-9) replaces the proposal in the Draft Summary of a permanent synod of bishops elected by episcopal conferences to support the Petrine ministry.[20]

17. See Okoye, "For a Synodal Church," 75.
18. Sarah and Benedict XVI, *From the Depths of Our Hearts*.
19. Mares, "Pope Francis Discusses Revising," §§4, 8–9.
20. In 1999, Cardinal Carlo Martini of Milan had dreamed of a permanent synodal church, with collegial and authoritative exchanges among all the bishops on some key issues. In 2004, he opined that the synod of bishops could fulfil this role in a less centralized form of church governance. See Pentin, "Permanent Synodal Church."

Episcopal conferences existed before Vatican II in an informal manner. For example, the Swiss Bishops' Conference was founded in 1863. Leo XIII in 1899 convoked a plenary Latin American Council of Metropolitan Bishops of the continent.[21] Vatican II encouraged their reinvigoration (*CD*, 18, 24). They were further defined by Pope Paul VI's 1966 Motu Proprio *Ecclesiae sanctae*. Today national episcopal conferences exist everywhere. Already the 1985 Extraordinary Synod stated that "the inalienable responsibility of each bishop in relation to the church, particular and universal, calls for deeper study of the theological and juridical status of episcopal conferences, especially the issue of their doctrinal authority" (IIc, 5). Saint John Paul II responded with his Motu Proprio *Apostolos suos* (see above).[22] On the other hand, Pope Francis hoped that "a juridical status of episcopal conferences would see them as subjects of specific attributions, including genuine doctrinal authority" (*EG*, 32).

The question of lay participation in the synod of bishops was hotly debated. When on April 26, 2023, the Synod Secretariat announced that Pope Francis had added non-bishops as voting members of this synod, though less than 25 percent of the membership, it carefully affirmed that this neither changed the nature of the assembly as synod of bishops nor contradicted the established norms. Some bishops, like Cardinal Müller, chafed at having only three minutes to speak to the whole assembly.[23] Some conservative theologians see lay participation as ending the episcopal and hierarchical nature of the synod of bishops.[24]

Not picked up in this document is the note in *DCS*, no. 34 lamenting the lack of the voice of priests and bishops speaking for themselves and their experience of walking together; also, *DCS*, no. 19 (Ep. Conf. Austria) of priests' exhaustion induced by the shortage of priests and the increasing loss of volunteers; "besides, they do not always feel heard, some see their ministry questioned."

---

21. ITC, *Synodality in Life of Church*, 39.

22. In particular, unanimous approval of the conference is demanded for any authentic magisterium.

23. See ch. 14 below, "Evaluations of the Synod Experience."

24. Fr. Murray, an EWTN commentator, opined that as the decision was made without a papal decree or any formal change in canon law, the general assembly of the synod and all its acts "would be subject to a technical complaint of canonical nullity." See Pentin, "Is It a Canonical Synod."

## APPROACH TO OPEN QUESTIONS

> This basic approach [listening first to the reasoning that supports the position of others] creates a context that enables careful consideration of matters that are controversial within the church, such as the anthropological effects of digital technologies and artificial intelligence, non-violence and legitimate self-defense, issues related to ministry, and issues related to sexuality and "bodiliness," among others (15, b; 336/10).
>
> In different ways, people who feel marginalized or excluded from the church because of their marriage status, *identity or sexuality* [italics mine] also ask to be heard and accompanied. There was a deep sense of love, mercy, and compassion felt in the assembly for those who are or feel hurt or neglected by the church, who want a place to call "home" where they can feel safe, be heard and respected, without fear of feeling judged. The assembly reiterates that Christians must always show respect for the dignity of every person (16, h; 326/20).
>
> We propose that initiatives enabling shared discernment on controversial doctrinal, pastoral and ethical issues should be developed, in the light of the Word of God, church teaching, theological reflection and an appreciation of the synodal experience. When appropriate it should also involve people directly affected by the matters under consideration (15, k; 310/36).[25]

## Commentary

Chapter 15 of the *Synthesis Report*, titled "Ecclesial Discernment and Open Questions," outlines the issues; chapter 16, titled "Towards a Listening and Accompanying Church," focuses on the persons concerned in these issues. The church may have sometimes too comfortably reiterated certain assertions without listening deeply to the persons concerned or attending to new experiences or facts.

---

25. "In the light of the Word of God, church teaching, theological reflection and an appreciation of the synodal experience" was added between the Draft Summary and *Synthesis Report*—an effort by conservatives to stress revelation and tradition. However, "should also involve people directly affected by the matters under consideration" sanctions the mere application of general principles.

The synod members overwhelmingly listened to the voices of those who have felt marginalized from the life of the church. As Pope Francis always says, the church is meant to announce the gospel to everyone (*todos, todos, todos*) and to gather them into the Body of Christ.[26]

The term LGBTQ was dropped between the Summary and the *Synthesis Report* because many delegates saw it as reflective of an ideology foisted upon countries by the West or a form of "neo-colonialism."[27] Besides, in some countries of the South, the same-sex lifestyle is proscribed by state and culture.

## EPISTEMOLOGY: FAITH AND REASON

> This [deeper criteria of ecclesial discernment] implies, first of all to specify the relationship between listening to the Word of God attested to in Scripture, the reception of Tradition and the magisterium of the church, and the prophetic reading of the signs of the times (2, f; 333/11).
>
> It is important to clarify how conversation in the Spirit can integrate the contributions of theological thought and the humanities and social sciences, alongside other models of ecclesial discernment that are used such as the "see, judge, act" approach or the steps of "recognize, interpret, choose" (2, h; 336/8).
>
> It is important to deepen the dialogue between the human sciences, especially psychology and theology, for an understanding of human experience that does not merely situate these approaches by side by side but integrates them into a more mature synthesis (14, h; 342/4).
>
> Certain issues, such as those relating to matters of identity and sexuality, the end of life, complicated marital situations, and ethical issues related to artificial intelligence, are controversial not only in society, but also in the church, because they raise new questions. Sometimes the anthropological categories we have developed are not able to grasp the complexity of the elements emerging from experience or knowledge in the sciences and require greater precision and further study. It is important to take the time required for

---

26. Barron, "My Experience of the Synod."

27. Martin, "What Happened." He wished that the *Synthesis* was more reflective of the rich conversation around the topic and admitted the divergences, as was done in other controversial areas.

this reflection and to invest our best energies in it, without giving in to simplistic judgements that hurt individuals and the Body of the church (15, g; 307/39).

## Commentary

The synod recognizes that differences in epistemology and methodology sometimes contributed to the tensions. Conversation in the Spirit may be great for helping people understand one another better, but it is not well-suited for careful or complex theological or practical reasoning (see comment of Fr. Anthony Lusvardi, SJ, above).

On faith versus science/reason, Pope Francis wrote: "Faith is not fearful of reason; on the contrary, it seeks and trusts reason, since 'the light of reason and the light of faith both come from God' (Aquinas, *Summa Contra Gentiles*, 14; John Paul II, *Fides et Ratio*, no. 43) and cannot contradict each other" (*EG*, no. 242).

The call for updating anthropological analyses in ethical matters will shake up moral theology going forward.[28] The struggle was already apparent in the various editions of the *Catechism of the Catholic Church* on homosexuality (no. 2357).

> 1994 edition
>
> The number of men and women who have deep-seated tendencies is not negligible. *They do not choose their homosexual condition, for most of them it is a trial* [italics mine].
>
> 1998 edition
>
> Its psychological genesis remains largely unexplained.

The impression given is that the psychological genesis does not matter, nor warrant further investigation in view of moral judgments.[29] Halík, on the contrary, insists that "the church's arguments, based on an ahistorical

---

28. Bishop Bätzing of the German Synodal Way comments, "When the synod says that previous formulations in the church's teaching on human beings are no longer sufficient here, and that they are moving forward at this point, also with support from science, then this is a huge step forward." Liedl, "'Pure Manipulation.'"

29. Bishop Barron rejects the idea that advances in science may affect moral teaching. "Evolutionary biology, anthropology, and chemistry might give us fresh insight into the etiology and physical dimension of same-sex attraction, but they will not tell us a thing about whether homosexual behavior is right or wrong." Barron, "My Experience of the Synod."

perception of unchanging human nature—ignoring, for example, the findings of medical science on homosexual orientation—have proved unconvincing."[30]

## A PASTORAL APPROACH MARKED BY TRUTH AND LOVE

> If we use doctrine harshly and with a judgmental attitude, we betray the Gospel; if we practice mercy "on the cheap," we do not convey God's love. The unity of truth and love implies bearing the difficulties of others, even making them our own, as happens between brothers and sisters. This unity can only be achieved, however, by patiently following the path of accompaniment (15, f; 336/10).
>
> Pope Francis said that the participation of baptized men and women living in complex situations of loving relationship "can be expressed in different ecclesial services, which necessarily requires discerning which of the various forms of exclusion currently practiced in the liturgical, pastoral, educational and institutional framework, can be surmounted" (*Amoris laetitia*, no. 299). This discernment also concerns their exclusion from parish and diocesan community participation bodies as experienced in some local churches (18, f; 311/35).
>
> The Symposium of the Episcopal Conferences of Africa and Madagascar (SECAM) are asked to "promote a theological and pastoral discernment on the question of polygamy and the accompaniment of people in polygamous unions who are coming to faith" (16, q; 303/43).

## Commentary

Eph 4:15–16 enjoins, "But speaking the truth in love, we must grow up in every way into him who is the head, into Christ" (see also Ps 85:11). The "perceived tension between love and truth" refers to "the Christological paradox of boldly proclaiming its authentic teaching while at the same time offering a witness of radical inclusion and acceptance through its pastoral and discerning accompaniment (*DCS*, no. 30).

Accompaniment enshrines Pope Francis' pastoral practice. As defined in *AL*, no. 297, it "is a matter of reaching out to everyone, of needing to

---

30. Halík, *Afternoon of Christianity*, 88.

help each person find his or her proper way of participating in the ecclesial community and thus to experience being touched by an 'unmerited, unconditional and gratuitous' mercy." Accompaniment calls for theological and cultural research "that takes as its starting point the daily experience of God's Holy People and places itself at its service" (15, j; 328/18).

On December 18, 2023, the DDF issued the Declaration *Fiducia Supplicans, On the Pastoral Meaning of Blessings*. It is not clear whether this theme was discussed in the assembly. The term *blessing* does not appear in the *Synthesis Report*, nor did it in that sense in *IL*.

## SEXUAL ABUSE IN THE CHURCH

> The church needs to listen with special attention and sensitivity to the voices of victims and survivors of sexual, spiritual, economic, institutional, power and conscience abuse by clergy members or persons with church appointments. Authentic listening is a fundamental element of the path to healing, repentance, justice and reconciliation (16, f; 339/7).
>
> Integral to a synodal church is ensuring a culture of transparency and respect for the procedures established for the protection of minors and vulnerable people. It is necessary to develop further structures dedicated to the prevention of abuse. The sensitive issue of handling abuse places many bishops in the difficult situation of having to reconcile the role of father with that of judge. The appropriateness of assigning the judicial task to another body, to be specified canonically, should be explored (12, i; 320/26).

## Commentary

Halík's comment on the sexual abuse is thought-provoking:

> The phenomenon of abuse is playing a similar role today to that of the sale of indulgences that precipitated the Reformation in the late Middle Ages. What at first seemed to be a marginal phenomenon, today—as then—clearly points to even deeper problems: the disorders of *the system*—namely, the relations between church and power, and between clergy and laity, among many others.[31]

---

31. Halík, *Afternoon of Christianity*, 65 (italics original).

# 13

## Toward the October 2024 Assembly

THE INTRODUCTION TO THE *Synthesis Report* laid out the task for the episcopal conferences:

> Taking their starting point from the convergences already reached, they are called to focus on the questions and proposals that are considered most urgent. They are asked to encourage a deepening of the issues both pastorally and theologically, and to indicate their canonical implications.

On December 11, 2023, the Secretariat of the Synod gave further details in a document, *Towards October 2024*, indicating the main topic to be "How to Be a Synodal Church on Mission." Episcopal conferences were requested to forward to the Synod Secretariat by May 15, 2024, a summary of not more than eight pages. On the basis of the material thus gathered, the *Instrumentum laboris* of the 2024 Second Session will be drafted.

On February 17, 2024, the General Secretariat of the Synod announced that the 2024 Synod will open on October 2 and end on October 27. It will be preceded by a two-day retreat, September 30 to October 1. The pope also announced the establishment of study groups to delve into some of the themes that had emerged last October in the first session of the synod. The study groups are to involve the dicasteries of the Roman Curia that have "specific competence" in relation to the particular theme under examination. They are to work in a synodal manner with the Secretariat of the Synod. Additionally, six more consultors for the General Secretariat of the Synod have been named, together with ten others named earlier.[1]

## THEMES FOR STUDY

On March 14, 2024, Pope Francis in a letter to Cardinal Grech indicated ten themes for study toward the October 2024 assembly. The General Secretariat of the Synod, in agreement with the competent dicasteries of the Roman Curia, is entrusted with constituting the study groups, in a manner that "calls pastors and experts from all Continents to be part of them and taking into consideration not only the studies that already exist, but also the most relevant experiences taking place in the People of God gathered in the local churches."[2] On the same date, the Synod Secretariat published a *Work Outline*, circumscribing the topic for each of the issues and indicating the groups involved in the study of each in collaboration with the Synod Secretariat. A report on the progress of this work will be presented at the Second Session in October 2024.[3] The groups should finish their work, if possible, by the end of June 2025.[4] In approving the lines of work, Pope Francis insisted, "The Synod is about synodality and not about this or that theme . . . The important thing is how the reflection is done, that is, in a synodal way."[5] Here are the ten themes.

> 1. Some aspects of the relationship between the Eastern Catholic Churches and the Latin Church (SR 6).
>
> 2. Listening to the cry of the poor (SR 4 and 16).
>
> 3. The mission in the digital environment (SR 17).
>
> 4. The revision of the *Ratio Fundamentalis Institutionis Sacerdotalis* in a missionary synodal perspective (SR 11).
>
> 5. Some theological and canonical matters regarding specific ministerial forms (SR 8 and 9).
>
> 6. The revision, in a synodal missionary perspective, of the documents touching on the relationship between bishops, consecrated life, and ecclesial associations (SR 10).

1. O'Connell, "Pope Francis Sets Dates."
2. Francis, "Letter of the Holy Father."
3. Secretariat of the Synod, *Towards October 2024*.
4. Secretariat of the Synod, *Work Outline*, no. 7.
5. Secretariat of the Synod, *Towards October 2024*.

7. Some aspects of the person and ministry of the bishop (criteria for selecting candidates to episcopacy, judicial function of the bishops, nature and course of *ad limina Apostolorum* visits) from a missionary synodal perspective (*SR* 12 and 13).

8. The role of Papal Representatives in a missionary synodal perspective (*SR* 13).

9. Theological criteria and synodal methodologies for shared discernment of controversial doctrinal, pastoral, and ethical issues (*SR* 15).

10. The reception of the fruits of the ecumenical journey in ecclesial practices (*SR* 7).

## PARISH PRIESTS TO MEET

Many in the synod assembly noted that parish priests were lacking among the participants. The priests in attendance tended to be religious superiors, professors, and experts helping with facilitation. In a Press Release on February 1, the Secretariat of the Synod announced a meeting of three hundred representatives of the world's parish priests to be held from April 28 to May 2 in *Fraterna Domus* in Sacrofano, near Rome, a meeting "of listening, prayer and discernment." On May 2, the parish priests met with Pope Francis and were able to have a dialogue with him.

They were selected by the world's 114 bishops' conferences and the 23 Eastern rite Catholic Churches. The selection had to be made by March 15, and the names were then sent to the Synod Secretariat.

They also sat at round tables. Their input will be forwarded to the Synod Secretariat, which will take them into account in drafting the working document (*Instrumentum laboris*) for the final session of the synod next October. As of the time of writing, there is no indication that any representatives of this group will be invited to that final session.[6]

---

6. Synod of Bishops, "Parish Priests for the Synod."

# 14

# Evaluations of the 2023 Synod Experience

ON OCTOBER 29, THE morning after the voting on the *Synthesis Report*, **Bishop Georg Bätzing**, president of the German Bishops' Conference, and other German bishops who had participated in the October 4–29 gathering held a press conference in Rome. Bishop Bätzing contended that the synod "echoed many of the issues that have been advanced by the German Synodal Way."[1] Thomas Söding[2] also saw in the synod "a confirmation of the Synodal Path in Germany . . . The issues we address are clearly issues that are important throughout the universal church."[3]

Pointing to the paragraph that "'the anthropological categories' used by the church to engage with contentious issues related to sexuality and identity are sometimes 'not able to grasp the complexity of the elements emerging from experience or knowledge in the sciences,'" Bishop Bätzing declared, "When the synod says that previous formulations in the church's teaching on human beings are no longer sufficient here, and that they are moving forward at this point, also with support from science, then this is a huge step forward."[4]

---

1. Liedl, "Pure Manipulation," §4.

2. The vice president of the Central Committee for German Catholics (ZdK), a powerful lay organization that has co-sponsored the German Synodal Way. He serves as a theological expert at this synod.

3. Liedl, "Pure Manipulation," §6.

4. Liedl, "Pure Manipulation," §§7, 10.

The first meeting of the so-called "synodal committee," the mixed body of bishops and laity, was November 10–11, 2023. The committee laid the groundwork for a permanent "Synodal Council" to govern the Catholic Church in Germany. The Synodal Council, which would allow laity to override bishops in decision-making, has been explicitly proscribed by the Vatican.

Four of Germany's twenty-seven diocesan bishops "voted to block funding for the synodal committee and will not participate."[5] On the other hand, the bishop of Speyer called for priests in his diocese to be open to blessing same-sex unions, including in Catholic churches.

**Cardinal Gerhard Müller**, a fellow German, left the synod three days early to ordain a priest in Poland. He warned that the synod on synodality was being used by some to prepare the church to accept false teaching. Some in the assembly, he felt,

> are "abusing the Holy Spirit" in order to introduce "new doctrines" such as an acceptance of homosexuality, women priests, and a change in church governance. . . . All is being turned around so that now we must be open to homosexuality and the ordination of women. If you analyze it, all is about converting us to these two themes. Some have this image of an "inverted pyramid" of governance, but at the center of this pyramid is the personal will of the pope, and of his advisers and collaborators. This can be an image for making clear to children, but a "pyramid" or "polyhedron" is not a biblical image of the church.[6]
>
> The assembly was "very controlled" and quite manipulated, with most of the interventions coming from only a few people who spoke to them as if they knew no theology. . . . He, himself, was given only three minutes to speak to the whole assembly. . . . The synod organizers yesterday reaffirmed it's a synod of bishops, but how can it be when lay people have the same voice, they have the same time to speak, and they take away opportunities for the bishops [to have] the possibility to speak? It's not in reality a synod of bishops but more like an Anglican understanding of a synod, with three chambers according to a worldly parliament. This is not the Catholic Church.[7]

---

5. Liedl, "Pure Manipulation," §19.
6. Pentin, "Cardinal Müller Says," §§2, 11–12.
7. Pentin, "Cardinal Müller Says," §§4, 18.

Asked whether he still saw the synod as a "hostile takeover" as he said beforehand, he answered,

> It's not clear. They don't say openly what they mean. They cannot say openly, "We want to contradict the Word of God." But they are introducing a new hermeneutic with which they want to reconcile the Word of God with these ideologies—anti-Christian ideologies. But we cannot reconcile Christ and the Antichrist. This homosexual, LGBT ideology is, at its center, an anti-Christian ideology. It's the spirit of the Antichrist speaking through them. It is absolutely against creation.[8]

**Cardinal Hollerich**, on the other hand, affirmed that the synod, "is about synodality... even if people have not believed us." He admitted that "sometimes people had their 'knives out' over an issue during small-group discussions at the Oct. 4–29 assembly," though "eventually an alternative solution would be discovered." "To have this freedom and openness will change the church." "It was clear to me that some topics would have resistance. I am full of wonder that so many people have voted in favor. That means that the resistance [was] not so great as people have thought before. So yes, I am happy with that result."[9]

**Cardinal McElroy** weighed in, "It was a grinding process because the level of engagement we needed for the Conversations in the Spirit, which were very rewarding, were also very demanding." "I don't think there should ever again be a synod of bishops which does not include non-bishops as voting members and lay people as voting members." The theological development of what this exact nature is and the relationship between primacy, collegiality, and synodality, in the sense of the whole People of God being present—that needs to be crystallized.[10]

**Cardinal Cupich** of Chicago asserted that

> the document [*Synthesis Report*] is not as important as the experience that the delegates had. It's a new way of being church. At the same time, the document does call for a codification of synods in the future along these lines, rather than going back to what we did before.... Looking at the question of being a pastor of a parish, which seems to link the one who presides at the Eucharist with actual leadership, one may ask, Is that a connection that is absolutely

---

8. Pentin, "Cardinal Müller Says," §21.
9. Brockhaus, "Cardinal Hollerich," §§2–3, 11.
10. O'Connell, "Cardinal McElroy," §§3, 10.

necessary? Or can there be a leader of a community who is not the presider at the Eucharist but still has the same responsibility, authority, and role within the community as a pastor would have?[11]

The issue of LGBTQ was indeed much discussed.

And how people identify their sexuality is broader than the letters LGBTQ. It also dealt with people who are in their second marriage. What was being conveyed in the synod discussions and what the document tried to pick up was, first of all, that we should not start just with condemnations . . . [rather] get to know people and realize that in many discussions we don't know a whole lot. We have to really be careful about going full forward and pronouncing on things because we believe that there's a violation of God's law or a church protocol. We really have to accompany people; nobody should feel excluded.[12]

**Father James Martin**, SJ, narrated his experience seeing everyone discussing things on an equal footing, with even the pope at a round table. He realized that the message of the synod was this method which could help the church immeasurably in a time of great polarization.

Many delegates objected to even using the term "LGBTQ," seeing it more reflective of an "ideology" foisted upon countries by the West or a form of "neo-colonialism" and focusing more on homosexual acts as "intrinsically evil." From my point of view, I wish that the *Synthesis* was more reflective of the rich conversation around the topic and admitted our divergences, as was done in other controversial areas.[13]

---

11. O'Connell, "Cardinal Cupich," §§3–4, 15.
12. O'Connell, "Cardinal Cupich," §§27–28.
13. Martin, "What Happened," §§17–18.

# 15

# Conclusion

IT IS EVIDENT THAT the results so far are not negligible. The superb facilitation by Cardinals Grech and Hollerich put everyone at ease. Everyone had the *parrhesia* to register their true beliefs and reasoned positions since the process created space for all points of view. The media blackout and the members' commitment to secrecy helped. The synod of bishops takes the pulse of the church and its mission. Much more than the resulting documents, participants go home imbued with the joys and sorrows of the whole church, friendships are made, partnerships between churches forged. One is struck by the consensus on matters of faith and issues that require further study. The percentage with which proposals passed stands out. The highest dissent was for women's access to diaconal ministry (277/69), followed by the call for deeper study concerning uncertainties surrounding the diaconate (286/61), then the call for reconsidering priestly celibacy (291/55), and considering case by case reinsertion of priests who left the ministry (293/53). Besides the two proposals on ministry for women which carried by 80 percent, the rest carried by 95 percent and over. This means that despite the noise of some, the church all over the world is well united on the journey.

A second comment is this. From the matters proposed for further study it is clear that the assembly had its own voice, sometimes calling for the rationale for and clearer explanation of some magisterial teachings or practices. Hence, the call for further clarification and/or updating of John Paul's teaching on episcopal conferences, and of Pope Francis' proposals on synodality, Conversation in the Spirit, "all ministerial church," lay voting members of the synod, and lay participation in governance in the church.

My third comment regards the seating in round tables,[1] which remains the most inspiring symbol of synodality and the best fruit of this synod, in the opinion of many. The *Synthesis Report* characterized this sitting arrangement

> as emblematic of a synodal way of being church and an image of the Eucharist, which is the source and summit of synodality, with the Word of God at the center. In a church that is living synodally, different cultures, languages, rites, ways of thinking, and realities can engage together and fruitfully in a sincere search for the Spirit's guidance (1, c).

Fourth is "Conversation in the Spirit," called the "synodal method." The necessary listening to others before speaking and the breaks for prayer highlight spiritual discernment in common, allowing participants to overcome prejudices. Even the German Synodal Way bishop, Franz Josef Overbeck of Essen, noted that the synod's "Conversation in the Spirit method" could be incorporated into the German Synodal Way's work going forward.

Fifth, the church does not have a mission, but *is* mission. Every baptized person is *ipso facto* a missionary. Baptism is the foundation for articulating anew the meaning, scope, and content of the church's mission or the criteria for its diverse expressions. The multiplicity of the dimensions of mission are to be harmonized in the perspective of integral mission promoted by *Evangelii nuntiandi* and taken up in *Evangelii gaudium* (IL, B 2.1). Halík considers bypassed "the traditional forms of mission aimed at 'converting nonbelievers.' A truly new evangelization, worthy of the name, has a difficult task today: to seek the *universal* Christ, whose greatness is often hidden by . . . our too narrow perspectives and intellectual categories."[2]

Sixth, Pope Francis' pastoral approach of mercy has provoked constructive debate. Pastoral guidance must become "accompaniment" of persons. Accompaniment "is a matter of reaching out to everyone, of needing to help each person find his or her proper way of participating

---

1. The Australian Episcopal Council of 2018–22 sat in table groups of about ten people, including a mix of bishops, priests, religious, and lay people. See the testimony of Msgr. Shane Mackinlay, Bishop of Sandhurst, Australia (Synod of Bishops, "XVI General Ordinary Assembly").

2. Halík, *Afternoon of Christianity*, 210. On page 201 he sees this mission in the ministry of *spiritual* accompaniment, for *everyone*, not just the faithful, also helping people in the search for meaning in life and the meaning of particular life situations.

in the ecclesial community and thus to experience being touched by an 'unmerited, unconditional and gratuitous' mercy" (*AL*, no. 297). It better incorporates conscience into the church's praxis in certain situations.[3]

My seventh comment concerns the future of moral norms. If "sometimes the anthropological categories we have developed are not able to grasp the complexity of the elements emerging from experience or knowledge in the sciences and require greater precision and further study . . . without giving in to simplistic judgements that hurt individuals and the Body of the church (15, g)," then a "Copernican revolution" is brewing in moral theology. Eschewing "the peddlers of cheap certitudes," experience and conscience will be given more latitude, while natural law will no longer be "based on an ahistorical perception of unchanging human nature."[4] The church, bound to fidelity to Christ, can confess lack of complete knowledge of an issue and yet bind the faithful to certain norms, while even more diligently searching for the full truth.

Eighth, even without much hope of priestly ordination of women, this synod can be termed "the synod of the women." Women will sit at all tables of planning and decision-making in the church, and are valued stakeholders in the formation of clergy. Fifty of them had the vote compared to thirty priests, who were mostly non-pastors of souls! Time is overdue to also *listen* to priests split between two identities—acting in *persona Christi*, and being an extension of his bishop—both articulated in *LG*, 28 (italics mine):

> *make him* [the bishop] *present* in a certain sense in the individual local congregations, and take upon themselves, as far as they are able, *his* duties and the burden of *his care*, and discharge them with a daily interest;
>
> *in the image of Christ* the eternal high Priest . . . *true priests* of the New Testament. Partakers of the function of *Christ the sole Mediator* . . . they exercise their sacred function especially in the Eucharistic worship or the celebration of the Mass by which *acting in the person of Christ* and proclaiming *his* Mystery.

---

3. For example, conscience, more than recognizing that a given situation does not correspond objectively to the overall demands of the gospel, "can also recognize with sincerity and honesty what for now is the most generous response which can be given to God, and come to see with a certain moral security that it is what God himself is asking amid the concrete complexity of one's limits, while yet not fully the objective ideal" (*AL*, no. 303).

4. Halík, *Afternoon of Christianity*, 209, 88. He continues, "On the threshold of the future, let us not even be afraid to say 'we don't know' with honesty and humility" (209).

Finally, this is definitely a "Synod of the Holy Spirit." "Conversation in the Spirit" is no mere tactic or method, rather a praxis that prepares the church for willing docility to the Holy Spirit. Pope Francis never wavers in his faith that the Holy Spirit indwells and guides the entire People of God. In discerning the Spirit lies safety for the church.

The synod on synodality is rewriting Catholic ecclesiology,[5] giving new emphasis to the trinitarian and pneumatological dimensions of the church: "the universal and local are present in each other in the church of Christ . . . an ecclesiological *perichoresis* in which trinitarian communion sees its ecclesial reflection."[6] Vatican II took us from church as *societas perfecta* ("perfect society"; Vatican I) to church as communion of churches (*communio ecclesiarum*). The pope as *pontifex maximus* ("supreme pontiff") alone with universal magisterium became again Bishop of Rome alongside the College of Bishops, Successors of the Apostles. When it reversed the order of chapters 2 and 3 of the draft schema on the Church, putting the People of God before the bishops, *Lumen gentium* inverted the pyramid and ushered in *communio fidelium* ("communion of the faithful") as foundational. It did not fully work out the implications, but stopped halfway with *communio hierarchica* ("hierarchical communion") and an ecclesiology of jurisdiction.[7] Pope Francis and the synod on synodality are working out the implications of *communio fidelium* where all the baptized have equal dignity and through their various charisms and gifts of the Spirit mutually empower one another for mission.

Did the synod achieve its goal? This question is better answered after the second session coming October 2024 and the pope's exhortation. However, the goal, *syn-odos*, journeying together, was largely attained:

> to plant dreams, draw forth prophecies and visions, allow hope to flourish, inspire trust, bind up wounds, weave together relationships, awaken a dawn of hope, learn from one another and create a bright resourcefulness that will enlighten minds, warm hearts, give strength to our hands. (*PD*, 32)

---

5. Cavadini, "Need for a Deeper Theology," agrees, though adversely: "In other words, 'synodality' is an ecclesiology, at least implicitly, a particular theology of the Church, which claims to be a development of *Lumen Gentium*."

6. ITC, *Synodality in the Life and Mission*, no. 60.

7. Rush, *Vision of Vatican II*, 214, put it this way: Vatican II, to complete Vatican I, started with *communio hierarchica*, discovered *communio ecclesiarum*, and ended with pervasive emphasis on *communio fidelium*.

## CONCLUSION

The delegates to the October 2024 assembly will, nevertheless, have to be more attentive to what is blossoming in the life of the church, avoiding the pitfalls.

> Temptations and pitfalls to be avoided include: seeing only the problems and fixating on them (we can miss the light if we focus only on the darkness); focusing only on structures; the temptation of conflict and division, or treating the synod as a kind of parliament in which one side must defeat the other; wanting to lead ourselves instead of being led by God. (*Handbook* 2.4)

The ultimate measure of success will be a new "commotion of Pentecost" set off by the Holy Spirit. "*If* [through the Spirit] *the church becomes truly a community of mutual empowerment, we shall speak with the authority of the Lord.*"[8]

---

8. Radcliffe, "3 October 2023: First Meditation" (italics original).

# Bibliography

Abbot, Walter M., ed. *The Documents of Vatican II*. London: Geoffrey Chapman, 1966.
Aleteia. Synod: "How over 1200 Amendments Changed the Final Synthesis." Aleteia.org, accessed Feb. 13, 2024. https://aleteia.org/2023/11/14/synod-how-more-than-1200-amendments-changed-the-final-synthesis.
Allen, Elise Ann. "Vatican, German Bishops Spar over Proposal for New 'Synodal Council.'" *Crux*, Jan. 25, 2023. https://cruxnow.com/vatican/2023/01/vatican-german-bishops-spar-over-proposal-for-new-synodal-council.
Arinze, Francis, et al. "A Fraternal Open Letter to Our Brother Bishops in Germany." *Catholic News Agency*, Apr. 11, 2022. https://www.catholicnewsagency.com/storage/pdf/fraternal-open-letter-to-brother-bishops-germany.pdf.
Barron, Robert. "My Experience of the Synod." *Word on Fire*, accessed Feb. 23, 2024. https://www.wordonfire.org/articles/barron/my-experience-of-the-synod/.
Beal, John P., et al., eds. *The New Commentary on the Code of Canon Law: Study Edition*. New York: Paulist, 2000.
Benedict XVI. "Motu proprio: *Ecclesiae unitatem*." Apostolic Letter, Vatican website, July 2, 2009. https://www.vatican.va/content/benedict-xvi/en/apost_letters/documents/hf_ben-xvi_apl_20090702_ecclesiae-unitatem.html.
———. "Motu proprio: *Omnium in mentem*." Apostolic Letter, Vatican website, Oct. 26, 2009. https://www.vatican.va/content/benedict-xvi/en/apost_letters/documents/hf_ben-xvi_apl_20091026_codex-iuris-canonici.html.
———. "Motu proprio: *Summorum Pontificum*." Apostolic Letter, Vatican website, July 7, 2007. https://www.vatican.va/content/benedict-xvi/en/letters/2007/documents/hf_ben-xvi_let_20070707_lettera-vescovi.html.
———. *Ordo Synodi Episcoporum*, with attached *Adnexum de modo procedendi in circulis minoribus*. Vatican website, Sept. 29, 2006. https://www.vatican.va/roman_curia/synod/documents/rc_synod_20050309_documentation-profile_en.html.
Bevans, Steve. "Revising Mission at Vatican II: Theology and Practice for Today's Missionary Church." *Theological Studies* 74 (2013) 261–83.
Brockhaus, Hannah. "The Synod on Synodality's Listening 'Method' Comes from the Jesuits." *Catholic News Agency*, Oct. 24, 2023. https://www.catholicnewsagency.com/news/255793/examining-the-synod-on-synodality-s-conversation-in-the-spirit.
———. "Cardinal Hollerich: The Openness of the Synod on Synodality 'Will Change the Church.'" *Catholic News Agency*, Oct. 28, 2023. https://www.catholicnewsagency.com/news/255853/cardinal-hollerich-the-openness-of-the-synod-on-synodality-will-change-the-church.

## BIBLIOGRAPHY

*Catechism of the Catholic Church*. New York: Doubleday, 1994. Revised 1998.

Cavadini, John. "The Need for a Deeper Theology of Synodality." *National Catholic Register*, Nov. 24, 2023. https://www.ncregister.com/commentaries/the-need-for-a-deeper-theology-of-synodality.

Cernuzio, Salvatore. "Il Papa: le critiche aiutano a crescere, ma vorrei che me le facessero direttamente." *Vatican News*, Jan. 25, 2023. https://www.vaticannews.va/it/papa/news/2023-01/papa-francesco-intervista-associated-press.html.

———. "Synod: Laymen and Laywomen Eligible to Vote at General Assembly." *Vatican News*, Apr. 26, 2023. https://www.vaticannews.va/en/vatican-city/news/2023-04/synod-synodality-general-assemblies-laypeople-eligible-vote.html.

Coccopalmerio, Francesco. "On Omnium in Mentem: The Basis of the Two Changes." EWTN, accessed Apr. 18, 2024. https://www.ewtn.com/catholicism/library/on-omnium-in-mentem-the-basis-of-the-two-changes-1227.

Comblin, José. *The People of God*. Maryknoll, NY: Orbis, 2004.

Congregation for Doctrine of the Faith. "Instruction *Donum veritatis*, On the Ecclesial Vocation of the Theologian." May 24, 1990.

de Souza, Raymond J. "10 Highlights of 'Praedicate Evangelium.'" *National Catholic Register*, accessed Jan. 31, 2024. https://www.ncregister.com/commentaries/10-highlights-of-praedicate-evangelium.

Dulle, Colleen. "The German Synodal Way, Explained." *America*, accessed Dec. 2, 2021.

Francis. "Address at the Ceremony Commemorating the 50th Anniversary of the Synod of Bishops." Vatican website, Oct. 17, 2015. https://www.vatican.va/content/francesco/en/speeches/2015/october/documents/papa-francesco_20151017_50-anniversario-sinodo.html.

———. "Address at the Opening of the Synod on Young People." Oct. 3, 2018.

———. "*Amoris Laetitia* [*The Joy of Love*]: On Love in the Family." Post-Synodal Apostolic Exhortation, Mar. 19, 2016.

———. "*Episcopalis communio*: On the Synod of Bishops." Apostolic Constitution, Sept. 15, 2018.

———. *Evangelii gaudium* [*The Joy of the Gospel*]: *On the Proclamation of the Gospel in Today's World*. Encyclical. Vatican City: November 24, 2013.

———. Holy Mass with the New Cardinals and the College of Cardinals: Opening of the Ordinary General Assembly of the Synod of Bishops." Homily, Vatican website, Oct. 4, 2023. https://www.vatican.va/content/francesco/en/homilies/2023/documents/20231004-omelia-nuovi-cardinali.html.

———. "Letter of the Holy Father to His Eminence Cardinal Mario Grech, 14.03.2024." Holy See Press Office. https://press.vatican.va/content/salastampa/en/bollettino/pubblico/2024/03/14/240314f.html.

———. "Moment of Reflection for the Beginning of the Synodal Path." Oct. 9, 2021. In *Instrumentum laboris* of the 2023 synod, no. 17.

———. "Opening of the Works of the XVI Ordinary General Assembly of the Synod of Bishops: 'For a Synodal Church: Communion, Participation and Mission.'" Address, Vatican website, Oct. 4, 2023. https://www.vatican.va/content/francesco/en/speeches/2023/october/documents/20231004-apertura-sinodo.pdf.

FSSPX News. "The Reform of the Curia and the Ecclesiological Paradoxes of Fr. Ghirlanda." Mar. 24, 2022. https://fsspx.news/en/news/reform-curia-and-ecclesiological-paradoxes-fr-ghirlanda-27604.

———. "The Synodal Path to a German National Church (10): First Working Document." Accessed Dec. 2, 2021.

Gagliarducci, Andrea. "Synod on Synodality 2023: Work Begins on the Final Text as Second Week Wraps Up." *Catholic News Agency*, Oct. 14, 2023. https://www.catholicnewsagency.com/news/255686/synod-on-synodality-2023-work-begins-on-the-final-text-as-second-week-wraps-up.

Gaillardetz, Richard R. *Ecclesiology for a Global Church: A People Called and Sent*. Maryknoll, NY: Orbis, 2008.

Ghirlanda, Gianfranco. "The Apostolic Constitution '*Praedicate Evangelium*' on the Roman Curia." *La Civiltà Cattolica*, May 6, 2022. https://www.laciviltacattolica.com/the-apostolic-constitution-praedicate-evangelium-on-the-roman-curia/.

———. "Universal Church, Particular Church, and Local Church at the Second Vatican Council and in the New Code of Canon Law." In *Vatican II: Assessment and Perspectives*, edited by René Latourelle, 2:233–71. New York: Paulist, 1989.

Giangravé, Claire. "Papal Critic Praises Dubia by Conservative Prelates as 'Heroic Act.'" *Religion News Service*, Oct. 27, 2023. https://religionnews.com/2023/10/27/papal-critic-praises-dubia-by-conservative-prelates-as-heroic-act/.

———. "Pope Francis Warns German Synodal Path Could Lead to Break with Rome." *America*, Nov. 21, 2023.

Granfield, Patrick. "The Church as *Societas Perfecta* in the Schemata of Vatican I." *Church History* 48.4 (Dec 1979) 431–46.

Hahn, Judith. "*Potestas incerta*: The Ambiguity of the Ecclesiastical Law on Power with Respect to Lay Leadership." *The Canonist* 13.2 (2022) 176–94.

Halík, Tomáš. *The Afternoon of Christianity: The Courage to Change*. Notre Dame: University of Notre Dame Press, 2004.

Hauck, Friedrich. "*Koinos*." In *Theological Dictionary of the New Testament*, edited by Gerhard Kittel and Gerhard Friedrich, 3:789–97. Grand Rapids: Eerdmans, 1965.

Hughes, John Jay. Review of *The Ratzinger Report*. *Theological Studies* 47.2 (May 1986) 311–14.

International Theological Commission. *Sensus Fidei in the Life of the Church*. Rome, 2014.

———. *Synodality in the Life and Mission of the Church*. Rome: Mar. 2, 2018.

Ivereigh, Austen. *Wounded Shepherd: Pope Francis and His Struggle to Convert the Catholic Church*. New York: Holt, 2019.

John Paul II. "Address to the Bishops of the USA." Vatican website, Sept. 16, 1987. https://www.vatican.va/content/john-paul-ii/en/speeches/1987/september/documents/hf_jp-ii_spe_19870916_vescovi-stati-uniti.html.

———. "Address to the Roman Curia." Vatican website, Dec. 20, 1990. https://www.vatican.va/content/john-paul-ii/it/speeches/1990/december/documents/hf-jp-ii_spe_19901220_curia.html.

———. "*Christifideles Laici*: On the Vocation and the Mission of the Lay Faithful in the Church and in the World." Post-Synodal Apostolic Exhortation. Vatican website, Sept. 30, 1988. https://www.vatican.va/content/john-paul-ii/en/apost_exhortations/documents/hf_jp-ii_exh_30121988_christifideles-laici.html.

———. "*Fides et Ratio*: On the Relationship between Faith and Reason." Encyclical Letter,. Vatican website, Sept. 14, 1998. https://www.vatican.va/content/john-paul-ii/en/encyclicals/documents/hf_jp-ii_enc_14091998_fides-et-ratio.html.

———. "Motu proprio: *Apostolos suos*, On the Theological and Juridical Nature of Episcopal Conferences." Apostolic Letter. Vatican website, May 21, 1998. https://

www.vatican.va/content/john-paul-ii/en/motu_proprio/documents/hf_jp-ii_motu-proprio_22071998_apostolos-suos.html.

———. "Motu proprio: *Ecclesia Dei.*" Apostolic Letter. Vatican website, July 2, 1988. https://www.vatican.va/roman_curia/pontifical_commissions/ecclsdei/documents/hf_jp-ii_motu-proprio_02071988_ecclesia-dei_en.html.

———. *Novo Millennio Ineunte.* Apostolic Letter. Vatican website, Jan. 6, 2021. https://www.vatican.va/content/john-paul-ii/en/apost_letters/2001/documents/hf_jp-ii_apl_20010106_novo-millennio-ineunte.html.

———. *Ordo Synodi Episcoporum, with, Adnexum de modo procedendi in circulis minoribus.* Vatican website, Sept. 29, 2006. https://www.vatican.va/roman_curia/synod/documents/rc_synod_20050309_documentation-profile_lt.html#RESCRIPTUM_EX_AUDIENTIA.

———. *Pastor Bonus.* Apostolic Constitution. Vatican website, June 28, 1988. https://www.vatican.va/content/john-paul-ii/en/apost_constitutions/documents/hf_jp-ii_apc_19880628_pastor-bonus.html.

———. "*Reconciliatio et paenitentia*: On Reconciliation and Penance in the Mission of the Church Today." Post-Synodal Apostolic Exhortation. Vatican website, Dec. 2, 1984. https://www.vatican.va/content/john-paul-ii/en/apost_exhortations/documents/hf_jp-ii_exh_02121984_reconciliatio-et-paenitentia.html.

———. "*Ut Unum sint*: On Commitment to Ecumenism." Vatican website, May 25, 1995. https://www.vatican.va/content/john-paul-ii/en/encyclicals/documents/hf_jp-ii_enc_25051995_ut-unum-sint.html.

———. "Theological Basis for the Synod of Bishops: Address to the Council of the General Secretariat of the Synod of Bishops." Vatican website, Apr. 30, 1983. https://www.vatican.va/roman_curia/synod/documents/rc_synod_20050309_documentation-profile_en.html.

Kasper, Walter. *The Catholic Church: Nature, Reality and Mission.* London: Bloomsbury, 2014.

———. "The Church as Communion." *New Blackfriars* 74.871 (May 1993) 232–44.

———. "On the Church: A Friendly Reply to Cardinal Ratzinger." *America* 184 (Apr 23–30, 2001) 8–14.

———. *Theology and Church.* New York: Crossroad, 1989.

KNA International. "Male and Female Lay Theologians May Now Perform Baptisms in German Diocese." *America*, Nov. 9, 2023. https://www.americamagazine.org/faith/2023/11/09/theologians-baptism-germany-246466.

Lamb, Christopher. "View from Rome: 10 Years of Pope Francis' Pontificate." *The Tablet*, Mar 11, 2023.

Lennan, Richard. "Communion Ecclesiology: Foundations, Critiques, and Affirmations." *Pacifica* 20 (Feb 2007) 24–39.

Liedl, Jonathan. "German Bishop at Synod on Synodality: Church Should Not Ignore 'Signs of the Times.'" *Catholic News Agency*, Oct. 21, 2023. https://www.catholicnewsagency.com/news/255772/german-bishop-at-synod-on-synodality-church-should-not-ignore-signs-of-the-times.

———. "'Pure Manipulation': Germans Continue Push for Radical Change after Worldwide Synod." *National Catholic Register*, Nov. 8, 2023. https://www.ncregister.com/news/germans-continue-push-for-radical-change.

## BIBLIOGRAPHY

———. "Synod on Synodality: What Changed between Draft and Summary Report?" *National Catholic Register*, Oct. 30, 2023. https://www.ncregister.com/news/synod-on-synodality-what-changed.

Ligier, Louis. "'Lay Ministries' and Their Foundations in the Documents of Vatican II." In *Vatican II: Assessment and Perspectives*, edited by René Latourelle, 2:160–76. New York: Paulist, 1989.

Mares, Courtney. "Pope Francis Discusses Revising Priestly Celibacy in New Interview." *Catholic News Agency*, Mar. 10, 2023. https://www.catholicnewsagency.com/news/253834/pope-francis-discusses-revising-priestly-celibacy-in-new-interview.

———. "Secrecy at the Synod on Synodality: What We Know about Delegates' Confidentiality Requirements." *National Catholic Register*, Oct. 6, 2023. https://www.ncregister.com/cna/what-we-know-about-secrecy-at-the-synod-on-synodality.

Martin, James. "What Happened at the Synod on Synodality." *America*, Oct. 30, 2023. https://www.americamagazine.org/faith/2023/10/30/synod-synodality-james-martin-246399.

McDonnell, Kilian. "The Ratzinger/Kasper Debate: The Universal Church and Local Churches." *Theological Studies* 63 (2002) 227–50.

Messori, Vittorio. *The Ratzinger Report: An Exclusive Interview on the State of the Church*. San Francisco: Ignatius, 1985.

O'Connell, Gerard. "Analysis: The Synod Is Not Vatican III. It's Pope Francis' Implementation of Vatican II." *America*, Oct. 4, 2023. https://www.americamagazine.org/faith/2023/10/04/pope-francis-synod-vatican-ii-246206.

———. "Cardinal Cupich on the Synod, Women Deacons, Giving Bishops Job Reviews and Why 'LGBTQ' Was Left Out of the Final Doc." *America*, Oct. 29, 2023. https://www.americamagazine.org/faith/2023/10/29/cardinal-cupich-synod-synodality-women-deacons-lgbt-bishops-246394.

———. "Cardinal Hollerich: 'The Synod Is Not Vatican III.'" *America*, July 14, 2023. https://www.americamagazine.org/faith/2023/07/14/vatican-cardinal-hollerich-interview-synod-vatican-iii-245688.

———. "Cardinal McElroy: There Should Never Again Be a Synod without Lay People as Voting Members." *America*, Oct. 31, 2023. https://www.americamagazine.org/faith/2023/10/31/cardinal-mcelroy-synod-synodality-246406.

———. "Pope Francis Appoints Colombian Bishop and U.S. Laywoman to Lead Vatican Office for Protection of Minors." *America*, Mar. 15, 2024. https://www.americamagazine.org/faith/2024/03/15/commission-protection-minors-bishop-ali-247519?utm_source=piano&utm_medium=email&utm_campaign=2928&pnespid=sqN1UDhaJaNBx.CQrW26EYuUth2sBMJpLO7knLI3qwdm5YRNNbq2CNWwSorgnMgrhypF1GSoZw

———. "Pope Francis Sets Dates for October Synod. Study Groups Will Examine First Session Themes." *America*, Feb. 17, 2024. https://www.americamagazine.org/faith/2024/02/17/pope-francis-october-synod-dates-247343?utm_source=piano&utm_medium=email&utm_campaign=2928&pnespid=tLZ6CytKNqgfyqedvzXrGsqdoRnwU5VrN7btmPVtsAZmAk.ONU59BuGIHrmSOVmiekPa7Fhp3g

Okoye, James Chukwuma. "For a Synodal Church: To Live Communion, Achieve Participation, to Open Herself to Mission." *Spiritan Horizons* 19 (Fall 2022) 67–83.

O'Malley, John. "The Millennium and the Papalization of Catholicism." *Catholic History for Today's Church* (2015) 7–13.

O'Riordan, Seán. "The Synod of Bishops 1985." *The Farrow* 37.3 (Mar 1986) 139–58.

Paul VI. "Address for the Start of the First Ordinary General Assembly of the Synod of Bishops." Vatican website, Sept. 30, 1967. https://www.vatican.va/roman_curia/synod/documents/rc_synod_20050309_documentation-profile_en.html.

———. *Evangelii nuntiandi*. Apostolic Exhortation, Dec. 8, 1975.

———. "Motu proprio: *Apostolica sollicitudo*, Establishing the Synod of Bishops for the Universal Church." Vatican website, Sept. 15, 1965. https://www.vatican.va/content/paul-vi/en/motu_proprio/documents/hf_p-vi_motu-proprio_19650915_apostolica-sollicitudo.html.

———. *Ordo Synodi Episcoporum*. Vatican website, 1966, 1969, 1971. https://www.vatican.va/roman_curia/synod/documents/rc_synod_20050309_documentation-profile_lt.html.

———. "*Regimini Ecclesiae Universae*: On the Roman Curia." Apostolic Constitution, Aug. 15, 1967.

Pentin, Edward. "Is It a Canonical Synod of Bishops or Not? Some Observers Express Their Doubts." *National Catholic Register*, Oct. 25, 2023. https://www.ncregister.com/news/is-it-a-canonical-synod-of-bishops-or-not-some-observers-express-their-doubts.

———. "Cardinal Müller Says Synod on Synodality Is Being Used by Some to Prepare the Church to Accept False Teaching." *National Catholic Register*, Oct. 27, 2023. https://www.ncregister.com/interview/cardinal-mueller-says-synod-on-synodality-is-being-used-by-some-to-prepare-the-church-to-accept-false-teaching.

———. "Permanent Synodal Church—A Progressive Jesuit Cardinal's Dream Come True." *National Catholic Register*, May 21, 2021. https://www.ncregister.com/blog/permanent-synodal-church-martini-dream.

Philips, Gérard. "*Lumen gentium*: History." In *Commentary on the Documents of Vatican II*, edited by Herbert Vorgrimler, 1:105–36. Freiburg: Herder, 1967.

The Pillar. "What Is the 'Lay Governance' Debate All About?" Sept. 1, 2022. https://www.pillarcatholic.com/p/what-is-the-lay-governance-debate-all-about.

Radcliffe, Timothy. "1 October 2023: First Meditation. Hoping against Hope." https://www.synod.va/en/highlights/retreat-for-the-participants-of-the-synodal-assembly.html.

———. "1 October 2023: Second Meditation. At Home in God and God at Home in Us." https://www.synod.va/en/highlights/retreat-for-the-participants-of-the-synodal-assembly.html.

———. "2 October 2023: First Meditation. Friendship." https://www.synod.va/en/highlights/retreat-for-the-participants-of-the-synodal-assembly.html.

———. "2 October 2023: Second Meditation. Conversation on the Way to Emmaus." https://www.synod.va/en/highlights/retreat-for-the-participants-of-the-synodal-assembly.html.

———. "3 October 2023: First Meditation. Authority." https://www.synod.va/en/highlights/retreat-for-the-participants-of-the-synodal-assembly.html.

———. "3 October 2023: Second Meditation. The Spirit of Truth." https://www.synod.va/en/highlights/retreat-for-the-participants-of-the-synodal-assembly.html.

Ratzinger, Josef. "The Local Church and the Universal Church: A Response to Walter Kasper." *America* 185 (Nov 19, 2001) 7–11.

———. "The Transmission of Divine Revelation." In *Commentary on the Documents of Vatican II*, edited by Herbert Vorgrimler, 3:181–98. New York: Herder, 1969.

## BIBLIOGRAPHY

Rush, Ormond. *The Vision of Vatican II: Its Fundamental Principles.* Collegeville, MN: Liturgical Academic, 2019.

Sarah, Robert, and Benedict XVI. *From the Depths of Our Hearts: Priesthood, Celibacy, and the Crisis of the Catholic Church.* San Francisco: Ignatius, 2020.

Schneider, Athanasius. "A New 'Synodal Church' Undermines the Catholic Church." *The Catholic Thing*, June 29, 2023. https://www.thecatholicthing.org/2023/06/29/a-new-synodal-church-undermines-the-catholic-church/.

Schönborn, Christoph. "Lessons from the Council of Jerusalem, the Church's First Synod." *America*, Nov. 10, 2023. https://www.americamagazine.org/faith/2023/11/10/schonborn-synod-council-jerusalem-246438.

Secretariat of the Synod. *Work Outline: Study Groups for Questions Raised in the first Session of the XVI Ordinary General Assembly of the Synod of Bishops to Be Explored in Collaboration with the Dicasteries of the Roman Curia.* https://www.synod.va/en/resources/documents/documents-for-the-third-phase/study-groups-for-questions-raised-in-the-first-session-of-the-xvi-assembly.html

———. *Towards October 2024.* Vatican, Dec. 11, 2023. https://www.synod.va/content/dam/synod/news/2023-12-12_towards-2024/ENG_Document_TOWARDS-OCTOBER-2024_XVI_II-Session.pdf.

Symposium of the Episcopal Conferences of Africa and Madagascar. "Document of the African Synodal Continental Assembly." Mar. 2023. https://www.synod.va/content/dam/synod/common/phases/continental-stage/final_document/AFRICA-EN.pdf.

Synod of Bishops. "Collection of Patristic Texts." https://www.synod.va/content/dam/synod/assembly/0410/XVI-AGO---ENG---COLLECTION-OF-PATRISTIC-TEXTS.pdf.

———. "Letter of the XVI Ordinary General Assembly of the Synod of Bishops to the People of God." Oct. 25, 2023. https://www.synod.va/en/highlights/xvi-general-ordinary-assembly-of-the-synod-of-bishops.html.

———. *Instrumentum laboris of the 16th Ordinary General Assembly of the Synod of Bishops.* Holy See Press Office, Oct. 2022. https://www.synod.va/content/dam/synod/common/phases/universal-stage/il/ENG_INSTRUMENTUM-LABORIS.pdf.

———. "Parish Priests for the Synod." Feb. 1, 2024. https://www.synod.va/en/news/parish-priests-for-the-synod.html.

———. *Preparatory Document for the 16th General Assembly of the Synod of Bishops: For a Synodal Church: Communion, Participation, and Mission.* Holy See Press Office, Sept. 7, 2021.

———. "Profile: Synod of Bishops." Vatican website, accessed Jan. 30, 2024. https://www.vatican.va/roman_curia/synod/documents/rc_synod_doc_20190314_profilo_en.html.

———. *Synthesis Report: A Synodal Church in Mission.* Rome, Oct. 28, 2023. https://www.synod.va/content/dam/synod/assembly/synthesis/english/2023.10.28-ENG-Synthesis-Report_IMP.pdf.

———. *Vademecum for the Synod on Synodality: Official Handbook for Listening and Discernment in Local Churches.* Rome: General Secretariat of the Synod, Sept. 2023.

———. *Working Document for the Continental Stage: "Enlarge the Space of Your Tent, Spread Out Your Tent Cloths Unsparingly, Lengthen Your Ropes and Make Firm Your Pegs" (Isa 54:2).* Rome: General Secretariat of the Synod, Oct. 2022.

———. "XVI General Ordinary Assembly of the Synod of Bishops: Document." https://www.synod.va/en/highlights/xvi-general-ordinary-assembly-of-the-synod-of-bishops.html.

*The Tablet.* "First Female Secretary General of Vatican City State Appointed." Nov. 13, 2021, 26.

Ureta, José Antonio, and Julio Loredo de Izcue. *The Synodal Process Is a Pandora's Box: 100 Questions and Answers.* Translated by José A. Schelini. Spring Grove, PA: American Society for the Defense of Tradition, Family, and Property, 2023.

*Vatican News.* "Pope Francis Responds to Dubia Submitted by Five Cardinals." Oct. 2, 2023. https://www.vaticannews.va/en/pope/news/2023-10/pope-francis-responds-to-dubia-of-five-cardinals.html.

Watkins, Clare. "Objecting to Koinonia: The Question of Christian Discipleship Today—and Why Communion Is Not the Answer." *Louvain Studies* 28.4 (2003) 326–43.

Weigel, George. "A Laborious and Vacuous Instrument." *First Things*, June 28, 2023. https://www.firstthings.com/web-exclusives/2023/06/a-laborious-and-vacuous-instrument.

Weil, Simone. *Waiting on God.* Translated by Emma Craufurd. London: HarperCollins, 1959.

Wimmer, A. C. "Cardinal Zen Expresses Concerns about Synod on Synodality in Leaked Letter to Bishops." *Catholic News Agency*, Oct. 4, 2023. https://www.catholicnewsagency.com/news/255535/cardinal-zen-expresses-concerns-about-synod-on-synodality-in-leaked-letter-to-bishops.

Zengarini, Lisa. "Joy for the Creation of New Bishops' Conference of the Amazon." *Vatican News*, Oct. 20, 2021. https://www.vaticannews.va/en/church/news/2021-10/bishops-conference-of-the-amazon-canonically-erected.html.

# Index

Acts of the Apostles, as synodal paradigm, 4–6
*Ad gentes*, 8–9, 114
American Society for the Defense of Tradition, Family and Property, 71–72
*Apostolica sollicitudo*, 1
Authority, lack of, 83

Baptism, as foundation of ecumenism, mission, and participation, 108–13
Becquart, Nathalie, Sister, 28
Benedict XVI (Pope), 21–23, 24, 27, 120
    see also Ratzinger, Joseph, Cardinal
Bishops
    attendance at Synod Assembly, 75–76
    college of, 1, 9, 12, 17, 19, 20, 29, 62, 66, 106, 138
    episcopal conferences, 20–21, 23
    role of, 64
    role of, as listener, 38
    role of, in church communion, 9–10
    role of, in synodality, 18–19
    role of, relations with religious, 110
    selection of candidates, 105, 130
    teaching authority and *sensus fidelium*, 36
    see also Synod of Bishops

Canon law, balancing authority and participation, 64–65, 66
Canonical sources, for Synod on Synodality, 20–35

Cardinals
    College of, 19, 29, 142
    Council of, 70, 104, 119, 121, 122
    of Dubia: Walter Brandmüller, Raymond Leo Burke, Juan Sandoval Íñiguez, Robert Sarah, Joseph Zen Ze-kiun, 78
    headed Congregations, 29
    pre-conclave meeting 2013, 27
CEAMA (Ecclesiastical Conference of the Amazon), 26
Celibacy, priestly, 95, 117, 118, 120, 121
*Christus Dominus* (CD), 1, 9, 19, 24, 122
Church, as missionary, 18, 25, 114–16
Church order, episcopate, 118–19
Clericalism, 43
Climate change, 41
*Code of Canon Law* (1983), 20–23, 24, 109
Communio, 9, 18, 138
*Communio ecclesiarum*, 9, 18
*Communio fidelium*, 18, 138
Communion
    Congregation for Doctrine of the Faith, 13–14
    discussion by working groups, 91–93
    diverse and vulnerable communities, 55–59
    ecclesiology of, 96, 138
    hierarchical, 33
    and mission, 51, 67
    and participation, 79
    and synodality, 18–19
    theme in *instrumentum laboris*, 54, 55–59

# Index

Communion (continued)
    Vatican II, foundation for, 8–10, 12–13
Communities, communion with diverse and vulnerable, 55–59
Communities, vulnerable, 55–56
Conferences, episcopal, 20–21, 23, 44, 122
    doctrinal competence, 20–21
    German Bishops' Conference, 69, 131–32
Congregation for Doctrine of the Faith (CDF), 13–14
Congregation for the Clergy, 25–26
Continental Assemblies, 46, 56, 59, 60–61, 63, 64, 67, 68
Conversation, 82
Conversation in the Spirit
    to build consensus, 91
    communion, mission and participation, 49
    criticism of, 72, 74
    formation for, 52
    image of, 53
    limitation of, 125
    listening, as synodal method, 95
    renewal of processes, 65
    synodal method, 86, 136, 138
    *see also* Holy Spirit
Council of Cardinals, 70, 104, 119, 121, 122
Council of Jerusalem, as 'Proto-Synod,' 5
Cupich, Blase, Cardinal, 133–34

De San Martin, Luis Marín, Bishop, 28
Deacons
    *see* Diaconate
Diaconate, 20–23, 25–26, 120–21, 135
Dicastery, changes to, 28–32
Discernment, as synodal method, 6, 37, 123–24
Discernment, synodal church (image), 53
Divine revelation, 78, 79

Eastern Catholic Churches, 56, 57, 66, 129
*Episcopalis communio*, 2, 23–25, 75
Episcopate
    *see* Bishops

Epistemology, on faith and reason, 124–26
Eucharist, 9, 45, 62, 72, 106, 110, 111
*Evangelii Gaudium*, 14
Evangelization, 14–15, 18, 25, 30, 60, 115, 136

Faith, 8, 15, 16, 124–26, 135
Families, 42, 43
Formation, for women, 110
Formation, new mindset, 65
Formation, on priests, 63, 97
    women in training of priests, 110
Formation, on synodality, 45, 51–52
Formation, *Synthesis Report* on, 117–18
Francis (Pope)
    Address regarding anniversary of Synod of Bishops, 17
    Address to Assembly, 99–100
    on communion, 79
    conception of synod, 87
    on divine revelation, 79
    *Episcopalis communio*, 23–25
    *Evangelii Gaudium*, 14–16
    homily and opening address, 87–88
    *Magnum principium*, 23
    on marriage, 79
    on mercy, 136–37
    on ordination of women, 79, 120
    *Praedicate Evangelium*, 27–32
    on repentance, 79–80
    response to *Dubia* Cardinals, 78–80
    response to German Synodal Way, 70–71
    Roman Curia, changes to, 27–32
    Synod on Synodality, 46–47
    at synod round table, **86**
    on synodality, 17
    *Traditionis Custodes*, 27
Friendship, meaning of, 82

German Synodal Way, 69–71, 94–95, 131–32
Gospel of Luke, 5
Governance, power of Church, 32–35
Grech, Mario, Cardinal Secretary of the Synod of Bishops, xix, 75, 88, 101

# Index

Handbook
    see *Vademecum for the Synod on Synodality* (Handbook)
Hollerich, Jean-Claude, Cardinal, 67, 76, 89, 91, 95, 133
Holy See, diplomatic personnel, 31
Holy Spirit
    baptism, 16, 18
    doubts about leading church, 98, 132
    Francis on, 87
    against ideology, 70
    as inspiration for missionary vocation, 116n12
    patristic texts of, 88
    as protagonist, 4, 52, 89
    synod of the, 138, 139
    see also Conversation in the Spirit
Homelessness, 81–82
Homosexuality, 125
    LGBTQ, 43, 56, 58, 72, 76, 103, 124, 134
    same-sex relationships, 43
Hope, 81

*Instrumentum laboris* (IL), 49–68
    on communion, 50–51, 54, 55–59
    formation, 51–52
    on mission, 50–51, 54–55, 59–64
    on participation, governance and authority, 55, 64–67
    review of, 67–68
    synodal discernment, 49–51
    theological foundations, 49–53
    worksheets, 54–67
Intercultural approaches, 42
International Theological Commission (ITC), 4, 16, 18–19, 28, 109, 111n6, 119

John Paul II (Pope)
    *Apostolos Suos*, 20–21, 122
    ordination of women, 79, 120

Kasper, Walter, Cardinal, 10, 12, 13, 34

Ladaria Cardinal Louis, 69
Laity, role of, 44

Leadership, renewal of, 44
LGBTQ+ community, 43, 56, 58, 72, 76, 103, 124, 134
Listening, as synodal method, 4, 17, 37, 38, 41, 50, 52n3, 94, 109, 123
    see also *Vademecum for the Synod on Synodality*
Liturgy, 23, 27, 45, 60
Love and truth, as synodal theme, 51, 68, 126
*Lumen gentium* (LG), 7–8, 118, 138

Magisterium, 21, 24, 99, 124
*Magnum principium*, 23, 32
Marginalized people, *Synthesis Report: A Synodal Church in Mission*, 105
Mark Cardinal Ouellet, 69
Marriage, definition of, 72, 78, 79
Martin, James, Father, 76, 134
McElroy, Robert Walter, Cardinal, 133
Mercy, 136–37
Ministry, 42, 52, 58, 60–61, 63, 105, 109–11
Ministry, ordained, 43, 44, 52, 55, 60, 63, 65, 117, 121
Mission
    baptized for, 43, 64, 109–12, 114, 136
    as canonical mandate, 33–34
    as center of synodality, 4, 18, 50–51, 59, 93
    discussion by working groups, 93–94
    pilgrim church, 8
    redefined, 67–68
    theme in *instrumentum laboris*, 54–55, 59–64
    theme for 2024 Second Session, 128, 130
Missionary, church as, 8, 14, 15, 114–16
Moral norms, future of, 137
Müller, Gerhard Ludwig, Cardinal, 76, 132–33

*Omnium in mentum*, 21–23, 120
Ordination of women, 44, 68, 78, 79, 112, 120, 132, 137
Oriental Catholic Churches, 39, 58, 75

# Index

Parish priests, 25–26, 43, 130
Participation, governance and authority, 55, 64–67, 95–98
Pastoral guidance, 126–27, 136–37
Paul VI (Pope), 1, 19, 23, 27, 116, 122
Permanent Synodal Council, proposal, 71
Persecution, 42, 57
Pietro Cardinal Parolin, 69
Polygamy
    polygamous marriages/unions, 43, 56, 58, 72, 126
*Praedicate Evangelium* (PE), 27–32
*Preparatory Document for the 16th General Assembly of the Synod of Bishops* (PD), 2, 4, 6, 36, 37, 67, 138
Priesthood, 21–23, 104
    for married men, 63, 70, 121
    priests who left and married, 43
    spreading the faith, 8
Priests, parish, 130
Priests, shortage of, 42, 65, 122

Radcliffe, Thomas, Father, 6, 72, 76, 81, 83, 91, 96, 98
Ratzinger, Joseph, Cardinal, 10–11, 16, 35
    *see also* Benedict XVI (Pope)
*Ratzinger Report*, 10–11
Reconciliation, 41, 98
Repentance, 78, 79–80
Roman Curia
    reform of, 27–32
    ordaining officers as prelates, 105

Schneider, Athanasius, Bishop, 72–73
Schools, theological, 63
SECAM (Symposium of the Episcopal Conferences of Africa and Madagascar), 47–48
Second Extraordinary General Assembly of the Synod of Bishops, 11–13
Seminary, renew curricula and formation of professors of theology, 52, 61, 63
*Sensus fidei*, 16–17, 18, 56, 111, 112, 113
Sexual abuse, in the church, 41, 58, 61, 69, 82, 83, 127

Synod
    challenges of, 40–45
    communion, 54, 55–59
    as community, 59–64
    consensus on faith, 135
    contrasted with concilium, 1
    delegate round tables, 3
    on formation, 117–18
    on the Holy Spirit, 4, 138
    *Instrumentum laboris*, 49–68
    liturgy, 45
    meaning of, 1
    mission, 54–55, 59–64
    as mission and missionary, 59–64
    need for new spirituality, 44–45
    participants, 38–39
    participation, governance and authority, 55, 64–67, 95–98
    priorities for the, 45–46
    resistance to, 40
    significance of round tables, 89
    theme of communion, 41
    working groups (*circuli minores*), 90–91
Synod, 2024 Session, 52, 128–30
Synod assemblies, and papal magisterium, 24
Synod Assembly, 2023 Session, 85–101
    amendments to Draft Summary, 100
    on authority, 83
    on conversation, 82
    Eighteenth General Congregation, 99–100
    evaluations of, 131–34
    First General Congregation, 88
    Fourth General Congregation, 91–93
    on friendship, 82
    German Synodal Way, 94–95
    on the Holy Spirit, 84
    on homelessness, 81–82
    homily by Pope Francis, 87
    on hope, 81
    opening retreat, 81–84
    participants, 75–77
    patristic texts used, 88
    seating arrangements, 85–86
    Sixteenth General Congregation, 98–99
    Sixth General Congregation, 93–94

# Index

*Synthesis Report: A Synodal Church in Mission*, 85
Twelfth General Congregation, 95–98
Twentieth General Congregation, 100
unique perspective of, 135–36
working groups on synod methodology, 90–91
Synod of Bishops
  codified in canon law, 1–2
  creation of, 1–2
  Francis on, 23–25
  instituted by Paul VI, 23
  lay participation, 122
  Letter of the XVI Ordinary General Assembly, 102–3
  Second Extraordinary General Assembly of the Synod of Bishops, 11
Synod on Synodality, canonical sources, 20–35
Synod on Synodality, criticism of
  American Society for the Defense of Tradition, Family and Property, 71–72
  Cardinals' skepticism, 78–80
  German Synodal Way, 69–71
  objections raised, 69–74
Synodal church
  characteristics of, 6, 17–18, 49–53
  on communion, 51
  communities, vulnerable, 55–59
  discernment, 61–62
  on formation, 51–52
  intercultural approaches, 42, 47, 48
  as mission, 67
  processes, structures, and institutions, 96
Synodal process
  Conversation in the Spirit (image), 53
  as dialogue, 38
  discernment, 86, 123–24, 136
  as inclusive, 39–41
  listening, 37
  objectives of, 36–37
  theological framework, 49–54
  youth participation, 42
  *see also* Conversation in the Spirit

Synodality
  baptism is the root of, 15
  as constitutive dimension of the church, 78
  Francis on, 17
  function of, 108–9
  grammar of, 89–90
  meaning of, 2–4, 40
  paradigms of, 4–6
  and respectful dialogue, 50
  round tables as symbol of, 136
  skepticism regarding, 71–72, 73
  structures and ecclesiastical processes, 18–19
  *Synthesis Report: A Synodal Church in Mission*, 108–9
*Synthesis Report: A Synodal Church in Mission*
  approved, 100
  baptism, as foundation of ecumenism, mission, and participation, 108–12
  bishops, relationships with religious, 110
  church, as missionary, 114–16
  church order, episcopate, 118–19
  conferences, episcopal, 122
  Conversation in the Spirit, 124, 125
  Council of Cardinals, 119, 121, 122
  diaconate, 120–21
  discernment, as synodal method, 123–24
  drafts of, 103–7
  epistemology, on faith and reason, 124–26
  final revisions, 106–7
  formation, 110, 117–18
  Francis, on priestly celibacy, 120
  lay participation, 122
  LGBTQ+ community, 124, 125
  marginalized people, 105
  meaning of ministry, 105
  ministry, 109–10
  ordination of women, 120
  outline of, 105–6
  pastoral guidance, 126–27

# Index

*Synthesis Report: A Synodal Church in Mission* (continued)
    priests, challenges for, 117, 118, 120, 121, 122
    role of women, 103–4
    *sensus fidei*, 111, 112, 113, 114
    sexual abuse, in the church, 127
    shortage of priests, 104
    synod, on formation, 117–18
    synodal method, discernment, 123–24
    synodality, 108–9

*Traditionis Custodes*, 27

Universal church, 13–14

*Vademecum for the Synod on Synodality (Handbook)*, 2, 36–39, 139
Vatican Council II, 7–10
    baptism, 8
    Church as missionary, 8
    on communion, 8–10
    *Ratzinger Report* on, 10–11
    sharing of gifts, 66

Weigel, George, Father, 73
Women in training of priests, 110
Women, ordination of, 44, 68, 78, 79, 120, 137
Women, participation in canonical processes, 110, 112
Women, as deacons, 23, 44, 62–63, 68, 73, 103–4, 110, 111–12, 120, 135

*Working Document for the Continental Stage (DCS)*
    absence of poor, 40
    challenges of injustice, 41
    church, changing structures and procedures, 45
    clericalism, 43
    climate change, 41
    criticism of the word 'process,' 72
    difficulty with meaning of synodality, 40
    on discernment, 41, 68
    episcopal conferences, 44
    Eucharist, limited access to, 45
    families of former priests, 43, 121
    family migration, 43
    healing of collective memory, 41
    laity and deacons, 41, 44
    leadership renewal, 44
    LGBTQ+ community, 43
    ministry, 44
    Missal (1962), limited access to, 45, 112
    ordination of women, 68, 120
    persecution of Christians, 41–42
    priest shortage, 42
    SECAM response to, 47–48
    sexual abuse by clergy, 41, 61
    synodality, in formation, 45
    synthesis of reports, 39–40
    three key questions, 45–46
    youth, 41
Working groups (*circuli minores*), 90–91, 100

Ze-Kiun, Joseph Zen, Cardinal, 73–74

www.ingramcontent.com/pod-product-compliance
Lightning Source LLC
Chambersburg PA
CBHW072137160426
43197CB00012B/2138